ROUTLEDGE LIBRARY EDITIONS:
ACCOUNTING

Volume 2

THE EVOLUTION OF BEHAVIORAL ACCOUNTING RESEARCH

THE EVOLUTION OF BEHAVIORAL ACCOUNTING RESEARCH

An Overview

Edited by
ROBERT H. ASHTON

Routledge
Taylor & Francis Group
LONDON AND NEW YORK

First published in 1984

This edition first published in 2014
by Routledge
4 Park Square, Milton Park, Abingdon, Oxon OX14 4RN
605 Third Avenue, New York, NY 10017

Routledge is an imprint of the Taylor & Francis Group, an informa business

British Library Cataloguing in Publication Data
A catalogue record for this book is available from the British Library

ISBN: 978-0-415-53081-1 (Set)
eISBN: 978-1-315-88628-2 (Set)
ISBN: 978-0-415-83456-8 (Volume 2) (hbk)
eISBN: 978-1-315-88654-1 (Volume 2)

The Evolution of Behavioral Accounting Research

An Overview

Edited by Robert H. Ashton

GARLAND PUBLISHING, INC.
NEW YORK & LONDON 1984

ACKNOWLEDGMENTS

The Impact of Budgets on People is reprinted by permission of the Financial Executive Institute, copyright © 1952. "Distinguishing Good from Not-So-Good Accounting Research" is reprinted by permission of Ohio State University, copyright © 1960. Material from *The Accounting Review* and *Studies in Accounting Research No. 17* is reprinted by permission of the American Accounting Association, copyrights © 1956, 1957, 1982. Material from *Accounting Research 1960–1970: A Critical Evaluation* is reprinted by permission of the Center for International Education and Research in Accounting, University of Illinois at Urbana-Champaign, copyright © 1973.

Library of Congress Cataloging in Publication Data

Main entry under title:

The Evolution of behavioral accounting research.

(Accounting history and the development of a profession)

Includes bibliographical references.

1. Accounting—Research—Addresses, essays, lectures.
2. Psychology, Industrial—Addresses, essays, lectures.

I. Ashton, Robert H. II. Series.

HF5630.E95 1984 657'.072 83-49435

ISBN 0-8240-6302-3 (alk. paper)

For a complete list of the titles in this series see the final pages of this volume.

The volumes in this series are printed on acid-free, 250-year-life paper.

Printed in the United States of America

Contents

Introduction

Many students of the accounting literature, especially those with an interest in the behavioral aspects of accounting, will recognize the following quotation:

> Let us now turn to that part of accounting which is related directly to the psychological reactions of those who consume accounting output or are caught in its threads of control. On balance it seems fair to conclude that accountants seem to have waded through their relationships to the intricate psychological network of human activity with a heavy-handed crudity that is beyond belief. Some degree of crudity may be excused in a new discipline, but failure to recognize that much of what passes as accounting theory is hopelessly entwined with unsupported behavior assumptions is unforgiveable.

This passage was written by Carl Devine,* one of the first accounting scholars to emphasize the behavioral implications of accounting. It is often mentioned as an important stimulus to the development of behavioral accounting research.

A number of other writings have also been influential in the development of this research, but some of them are much less well-known or widely distributed than the Devine article. Some contributions that fit this description are included in this anthology.

The principal item reproduced here is Chris Argyris's classic monograph, *The Impact of Budgets on People,* published in 1952. This work, which has been out-of-print for several years, is considered by many to mark the beginning of behavioral research in accounting. It is followed by Robert Anthony's little-known critique of the general state of accounting research in 1960, which includes a brief critical evaluation of Argyris's research as well as some other behavioral studies.

The third selection was written by the American Accounting Association's Committee on Cost Concepts and Standards, and published in 1956. One section of that report dealt with the use of

*"Research Methodology and Accounting Theory Formation," *The Accounting Review* (July 1960), p. 394.

costs as a motivational device. This selection is followed by a 1957 article by Robert Anthony, who had been a member of the Committee, which elaborates on that section of the Committee's report.

Much of the research activity in the behavioral aspects of accounting during the 1960s and early 1970s is critiqued in the article by David Green, published in 1973. This article and the two responses to it, by William Bruns and Jacob Birnberg (also included), raise most of the concerns that behavioral accounting researchers and others had about this type of research in its "early" years.*

The final selection, excerpted from my own research monograph published by the American Accounting Association in 1982, provides a more comprehensive perspective on the development of behavioral accounting research, and it includes the period following Green's critique. It discusses the bifurcation of behavioral accounting research into two branches: (1) the impact of budgets and management control systems on the attitudes and performance of individuals subject to their control, and (2) the impact of accounting information on the decision making behavior of internal and external users. It also explains how the focus of behavioral accounting research changed over the years as later researchers heeded many of the criticisms of the earlier observers.

Robert H. Ashton
New York City
November 1983

*Many of the comments made by Green, Bruns and Birnberg relate to a book of readings, *Accounting and Its Behavioral Implications,* edited by William Bruns and Don DeCoster and published in 1969. The table of contents from that book as well as two additional evaluations of it—by Nicholas Dopuch and Selwyn Becker—appeared as appendices to Green's article and are reproduced here.

THE IMPACT OF BUDGETS ON PEOPLE

prepared for
CONTROLLERSHIP FOUNDATION, INC.

Under the direction of Schuyler Dean Hoslett
by
CHRIS ARGYRIS

with the assistance of
FRANK B. MILLER, JR.

THE IMPACT OF BUDGETS ON PEOPLE *was supervised from its earliest planning stage until the final manuscript was completed by a panel of the following members of Controllers Institute:*

CHARLES E. DYKES — *Controller, Cooperative G.L.F. Exchange, Inc., Ithaca, N. Y.*

T. P. GEDDES — *President, Great Lakes Forwarding Corporation, Buffalo, N. Y.*

JOHN H. GOODWIN, JR. — *Secretary & Treasurer, Columbus McKinnon Chain Corp., Tonawanda, N. Y.*

J. K. HILL — *Vice President & Treasurer, The Norwich Pharmacal Company, Norwich, N. Y.*

H. A. KETCHUM — *Controller, Fasco Industries, Inc., Rochester, N. Y.*

H. S. KUHNS — *Secretary & Treasurer, The Haloid Company, Rochester, N. Y.*

NORMAN OLLEY — *Controller & Secretary, The R. T. French Company, Rochester, N. Y.*

C. R. TUCKERMAN — *Secretary, Oberdorfer Foundries, Inc., Syracuse, N. Y.*

WILLIS T. WINDLE — *Treasurer & Controller, The Carborundum Company, Niagara Falls, N. Y.*

·FOREWORD

For many years managements have been developing techniques to help them plan and control the complex operations of the business corporation. Controllers have played a large part in the development of some of these tools—cost accounting, budgeting, special statistical studies and other techniques. Many of these tools have reached a state of considerable refinement. Some indeed have reached the ultimate state of dwelling within an electronic tube and emerging only to shake a mechanical finger at erring human beings.

In spite of this unquestioned progress, there is more and more evidence that making the tool is a far easier task than learning how to use it.

Budgeting is apparently such a management tool, and many controllers suspect that the difficulties in using it have been underestimated, if we may judge by the strong vote of interest they gave to this study when it was submitted on January 15, 1951 to the Controllers Institute members as a prospectus sheet, "The Human Factors in Budgets".

This report turns the spotlight upon the point at which men and budgets meet. By the very fact of the emphasis placed here upon problems of salesmanship and human relations, the report is designed more for staff members in the controller's department—and especially the budget unit—than for the controller himself. The average controller would not have reached his present status as part of the management team, if he had not possessed a far greater degree of salesmanship and insight into human reactions, than the average employee in the accounting phase of corporate management.

For this reason the verbatim responses and vigorous reactions of factory foremen and supervisors were recorded exactly as given. They are published here undiluted—after merely brushing off some of the mud carried in by earthy words.

They do not necessarily represent the views of Controllership Foundation nor of the majority of controllers any more than a daily newspaper interview with a politician or foreign visitor represents the viewpoint of the publisher of a newspaper.

We hope the report sheds light on one of the most basic "Control" questions faced by management — how to gain acceptance — real acceptance of standards and goals. If it serves to stir in some readers a few qualms of doubt as to how their budgets are really faring at the hands of supervisors, it will have served its purpose.

The research was coordinated and the report edited by T. F. Bradshaw, Research Director of the Foundation.

Walter Mitchell, Jr.

Managing Director

March, 1952

TABLE OF CONTENTS

Part I

INTRODUCTION

- How this Study Came About
- What this Study Tries to Do
- How the Research Task Was Accomplished
- Some Limitations of the Study

1

THE IMPACT OF BUDGETS ON PEOPLE

HOW THIS STUDY CAME ABOUT

PERHAPS ONE OF THE MOST IMPORTANT developments which has occurred in the industrial world during the past decade has been the great emphasis upon, and interest in, human relations. Almost every businessman's magazine contains at least one article or news item on this subject. As a result of this interest, new areas for study have been opened up and systematic studies have given management many insights for understanding human beings in their work environment.

Controllership Foundation has been aware of these developments. Some time ago it polled its membership regarding the need for conducting some research in the area of the reactions to budgets of those who use them. The response to the inquiry indicated a very real interest on the part of the membership in the human factors associated with or caused by budgets; a substantial majority of those responding to the question believed that research on the problem should be undertaken.

Therefore Controllership Foundation, as the research arm of the Controllers Institute of America, approached Dean Paul M. O'Leary of the School of Business and Public Administration at Cornell University in June 1951, with a request that the School conduct an exploratory study on human factors in budgets. The School agreed to do this and appointed Dr. Schuyler Dean Hoslett as project director, Dr. Chris Argyris as research associate in charge of the field work and analysis of the data, and Frank Miller as research associate to aid in the field work.

In keeping with the established policy of the Controllership Foundation, an advisory panel of Controllers Institute members was set up to assist the research team in its work. Members of the panel were consulted before the field work was begun and criticized the manuscript in the process of preparation. The research team wishes to express here its appreciation of the advice and counsel of the members of the advisory panel of Controllers Institute.

Thanks are also due to Robert C. Tyo of Porter-Cable Machine Company, Syracuse, New York, and to Edward N. Vanstone of Moore Business Forms, Niagara Falls, New York, who assisted in planning the project and to William F. Whyte of Cornell University, and Thomas G. Spates of Yale University who read and criticized the manuscript in draft form.

WHAT THIS STUDY TRIES TO DO

The purpose of the study is to examine problems and to raise questions concerning the possible *human relations* effects budgets have upon *supervisors*. Because of the nature of the problem this study cannot present final solutions to problems, nor answer questions in any definitive way. It can merely define a wider aspect of the budget problem and suggest possible solutions. Each controller must light up these approaches with his own experience. In short, this study, the first of its kind attempted by the Foundation, is primarily exploratory.

Because of the indefinable limits of the human problems in this area, the research team decided to focus its attention on how the supervisors feel about budgets and how the finance people feel about the same budgets. The group sought answers to questions such as these:

1. How do the finance people see their job?

2. What problems do the finance people see in relation to factory people? What problems don't they perceive?

3. Similarly, how do the factory supervisors see their job?

4. What problems do factory supervisors perceive in relation to the finance people

and/or budgets? What problems don't they perceive?

5. What similarities and differences exist between factory people and finance people with regard to values, attitudes, and feelings toward budgets?

It should be pointed out that due to the exploratory nature of the study no recommendations could be made to the managements of the plants studied, which could then be observed in action, checked, and analyzed by the research team. Therefore, it is extremely difficult to present many recommendations based solely upon these findings. There is, however, a growing body of practical suggestions developed in other research work which is relevant to some of the problems unearthed by this report. In our recommendations we have drawn upon these suggestions because they are relevant and, we hope, useful to the controller.

HOW THE RESEARCH TASK WAS ACCOMPLISHED

The problem of human factors in the use of budgets is an extremely difficult one. Not only is the subject of budgets *per se* complicated, but, to make matters more difficult, budgets are so closely interrelated with the other parts and functions of organization that it would be an immense task to study carefully and thoroughly the problem as a whole.

With the limited funds, time, and personnel available, it was decided to limit the study to budgets that evaluate factory supervisors continuously (i.e., weekly, bi-weekly, or monthly). The report primarily considers those manufacturing budgets such as production budgets, waste budgets, and error budgets which make a direct evaluation of the line supervisors.

In order to obtain the basic data out of which this report is built, operating and finance supervisors were interviewed in four plants. Coverage was extremely high: in Plant A, 90% of the factory supervisors and 85% of the finance supervisors were interviewed; in Plant B, 100% of each; in Plant C, 75% of factory supervisors and 50% of finance supervisors; and in Plant D a 25% sample of each.

The interviews were "nondirective" whenever possible; that is, each one interviewed was permitted to define the interview according to his desire. If he had some ideas on the subject which he wished to express, he was permitted to do so. If he did not have anything specific in mind, a scheduled interview was conducted on the basis of the schedule of problem areas predefined by the research team.

The four plants selected do not in any way represent a sample of industry either as to size, type or location. Some of the characteristics of these four plants may be helpful to the reader in assessing the results:

1. In each of the four plants there is a work force of no more than 1500 employees.

2. Plants B, C, and D are branch plants of a parent organization; Plant A is not.

3. Each plant manufactures a different product and each makes "custom made" products as well as products for stock.

4. The plants are located in relatively small towns (i.e., none is in a town of over 100,000 people).

5. The type of labor in each plant includes all levels from highly skilled to nonskilled.

6. All four plants are unionized.

The process of preparing manufacturing cost budgets is much the same in all four companies. In all cases the process starts with a meeting of the controller, the assistant controller and a top management group to determine over-all financial goals for the company in the forthcoming year. The controller's staff then translates the financial goals into the detailed cost breakdowns required for departmental budgets. This preliminary budget is sent to all superintendents who are asked to scrutinize the budget carefully and report any alterations they wish made.

Once the superintendents have their budget modifications clearly in mind, a meeting is held with the controller and his staff. Both parties come to the meeting "armed to the teeth" with ammunition to back their demands. After the disagreements are resolved, all parties sign the new budget proposal. The superintendents return to their offices, awaiting the new budget and the expected drive to "put it over."

SOME LIMITATIONS OF THE STUDY

Any study whose approach is purely exploratory must be conducted within the limits of fairly well-defined boundaries. These are some of the more important limitations imposed upon this study by its exploratory nature:

1. None of the plants studied has a supervisory incentive system as a part of its budget system. This seems a serious limitation and points to the need for further research.

2. The report does not include any material concerning the effects budgets have upon the workers in the plant. Casual interviews with workers suggested that they are definitely affected. How much they are affected, and through what channels, is not clear. This problem also deserves further study.

3. Budgets constitute only one of the evaluation processes management uses. As is commonly known, most evaluation processes tend to have "two strikes against them" simply because they tend to set goals for, and make evaluations of, the supervisors. As such, budgets do not escape the usual complaints. Moreover, it appears that many complaints are focused upon the budget because the budget is one of the few evaluation processes that is always in writing, and therefore concrete. Thus, some of the supervisors tend to use it as a "whipping post" in order to release their feelings about many other, and at times totally unrelated, problems.

   Because budgets are used as whipping posts, the comments presented in this report may have a negative "tone." It would have been appropriate to make small "side-studies" of the amount of complaining about the budget that is in reality complaining about other problems. Due to the limitations of the study, this was not possible.

4. Because of the confidential nature of some of the material much important information must remain "in hiding." It would be valuable, for example, to paint a clear, precise picture of the actual budget processes and how they are put into effect in each plant. This could not be done without violating confidences. Nor could the various supervisors who play a part in the budget process be more specifically identified.

Within the boundaries set by these limitations the problems mentioned in this study are probably valid in other plants when the budget system is used frequently and forcefully by top management (either finance and/or factory) to motivate, to "pressure," and to evaluate factory supervisors.

Part II

WHAT BUDGET PEOPLE THINK OF BUDGETS

What Budget People Think Are:

- The Use of Budgets
- The Differences Between Their Outlook and That of Factory Supervisors
- Their Problems with Factory Supervisors
- Some of the Solutions to these Problems

5

What Budget People Think Are:

THE USE OF BUDGETS

To the budget people, budgets have an extremely important function in the organization as the "eyes and the ears of the plant." They provide the answers to most questions and the budget people see themselves as the "answer men" of the organization. Consider the following examples:

> First let me say that budgets are the watchdog of this company. What do I mean by that? Two things: First, if we have profit, there's no problem; Second, if we are losing money, what can we do about improvement—any kind of improvement?

> We guard the fields. The budget department has to constantly strive to improve the goods and make the plant better. *There is always room to make things better.*

> Well, where would they [*management*] be without our information? *That's why we're the backbone of the company.*

The budget people, therefore, see their task as one of always examining, always analyzing, always looking for new ways to make the plant more efficient. Such a task is primarily a critical one. Its primary emphasis seems to be, "never be completely satisfied." One budget staff man described this as follows:

> Ours is a tough job. The function of budgets is to be critical. Budget people should never be satisfied. They should always try to find new and better ways of doing things.

There is, therefore, an important emphasis made on budget people *constantly finding things that are "sour,"* looking for weaknesses and, in general, looking for things that are *wrong*, not right.

Another emphasis is equally important. All the budget people interviewed insisted that the errors found and the weaknesses uncovered should immediately be sent to top management.

> If I see an inconsistency, I'll go to *top management* and report it. No, I never go to the supervisor in charge. It is our job to report any inconsistencies to the top management.

Once the information is in top management's hands, it is up to it to take action. In other words, budget results are primarily *top management* control instruments.

Consider some typical comments made concerning the emphasis on reporting the results to top management:

> You might say a *good* budget man is one who keeps his eye on the pulse of the factory and lets management, *top management*, know if anything is wrong.

> Budgets are an important tool for top management. They guide top management in its operations and measure what the plant has been doing. Also, they provide a ruler by which top management can figure out the expectations for coming production.

> I send all my reports to top management. That's where they belong. Then it does with it what it wishes.

Coupled with the task of finding weaknesses and reporting them to top management is a third emphasis on *doing the reporting soon.* Budget results can be effective only when they are "hot off the griddle." Whatever pressure budgets may generate to "motivate" a factory man to better his record would be lost if action was not taken immediately.

> It's our philosophy that we've got to get these figures to top management when they're hot. They're no good when the job is cold. As it is now, with our records, top management can get the factory supervisors together and *do* something right away.

A fourth emphasis is on using the budget as a means for putting pressure on operating supervisors.

> As soon as we examine the budget results and see a fellow is slipping, we *immediately* call the factory manager and point out, "Look Joe, you're behind on the budget. What do you expect to do about it?"

> True, he may be batting his brains out already on the problem, but our phone call adds a little *more pressure*—er—well, you know, we let them know we're interested.

> The important thing for us to do is follow up. The supervisor's interest lags unless someone is *constantly checking up on him.* A little pressure. If you don't, the tendency is to lag. You can't blame supervisors. They are interested in the machines.

> I think there is a need for more pressure. People need to be needled a bit. I think man is inherently lazy and if we could only increase the pressure . . . I think budgets would be more effective.

There can be no doubt that budget people realize budgets are management instruments by which pressure can be applied to the lower echelons for increased productivity and efficiency. The budget people, therefore, visualize themselves as being responsible not only for uncovering errors and reporting them quickly to top management, but also for providing figures which are used by top management to apply pressure to factory personnel.

Finally, budget people believe that budgets present a *goal*, a *challenge* to factory people. They think that without budgets factory people would have nothing "to shoot for"—would lack the help of a great motivating instrument. For example:

> Production budgets set the goals. The budgets, yes, the budgets, set a challenge for those fellows [*factory*]. It's something for them to shoot for. They need something to shoot for. All of us need a goal.

> Budgets serve as a *constant* reminder that a goal *has* to be met. Budgets help to make the people work and strive to meet the goal.

> All I can say, if they [*factory*] had nothing to guide them, where would they be? There would be all sorts of ups and downs. Budgets serve to set a goal for manufacturing. It helps them meet a challenge. Keeps them on a certain level. But as I said before, it gives them a goal.

In summary, budget personnel see budgets as performing at least the following important functions:

1. They are a means to make things better. There is always room for improvement. Inconsistencies, errors, weaknesses are constantly being discovered, examined, and reported to top management.

2. Properly used, they are a means of instituting improvements quickly. Budgets are of most value when their results are in the hands of top management as soon as possible.

3. They are a means of putting pressure on factory supervisors.

4. They provide a goal, a motivating force for the factory people.

What Budget People Think Are:

THE DIFFERENCES BETWEEN THEIR OUTLOOK AND THAT OF FACTORY SUPERVISORS

If the budget people see any important differences between the outlook of operating people and themselves, such information should be of value in ascertaining how "basic" are the causes of misunderstanding between the budget and production parts of the organization.

The results indicate that budget people see some very basic differences. For example:

> I would say that factory people have a different outlook on life. They tend to be more liberal toward others.

> The financial people, on the other hand, look at life more coldly. To them, it's all figures. The only thing they look at is what amount of money is involved. It's the total figure that counts.

> The factory supervisors' outlook on things is different. They emphasize *today*. Yes, they're looking at only the short run. We have to look at things in the long run. We have to see the whole unit. They worry about their individual departments.

> I think you'd almost say there are personality differences between factory and finance. We [finance] tend to approach everything with figures. We have to. We've been trained that way. Factory people approach it without worrying about costs.

> Yes, there are differences. We [finance] have been trained to see things as they are—to study them logically and systematically. We've been trained to look at a problem and say, "Well, *this is it*, one, two, three, bang, that's it."

The differences described above may be clues for understanding the human problems that arise. For example, if the factory supervisors are, in fact, only interested in the short run and if the budget staff does not see the short run as being crucial, then trouble will arise. Similarly, if the budget staff has a basically different outlook on problems from the factory supervisors, this difference will tend to increase disagreements.

What Budget People Think Are:

THEIR PROBLEMS WITH FACTORY SUPERVISORS

The budget people were asked to describe what they felt was the most difficult problem they faced in their relationships with factory supervisors. The majority of the replies fell into a very consistent pattern. The most pressing problem was "selling" budgets to factory supervisors. The budget people believed that the task was almost insurmountable. It was interesting to see that the three most often stated reasons for this problem with factory supervisors were (a) lack of education on the part of factory supervisors, (b) lack of interest, and (c) misunderstanding and/or mistrust of budgets. For example:

> I guess our biggest problem with factory supervisors and budgets is to get them to follow through with the budget and keep after their people. I guess many, not all, supervisors just don't pay enough attention to budgets. I can see where it might be difficult for our supervisors to understand budgets. Some just don't have the training. Of course, part of the cause is that supervisors don't understand budgets.

> There is no doubt in my mind that the big problem we have is to get their interest in budgets. If the factory man happened to be in finance before, then things would be all right. But if not, it's a *job* to get them to use budgets.

> One of the most important problems we have with budgets is that our supervisors don't know much. They are quite illiterate and that, of course, makes quite a problem for us.

> But I'll tell you what I think the big problem is: The factory fellows think that the office guys are just no good and they [*finance*] are always trying to put one over on the factory people. I think the big problem is to convince them that we're not out to cheat them, that the budget people are interested in fair and equitable budgets.

What Budget People Think Are:

SOME OF THE SOLUTIONS TO THESE PROBLEMS

Most of the solutions suggested by budget people seem to revolve around educating, or training, factory people in the appreciation and use of budgets.

These are some of the suggestions:

1. Supervisors should be taught the *use* and *need* for budgets in the company and specifically in their departments.

2. If possible, budgets should be explained so the supervisor would know exactly how and why budgets are constructed the way they are. (Most finance people were quick to caution against overwhelming the factory man with minute details of financial "buzz words." They all pointed out that the explanations should be kept as simple as possible.)

3. Closely connected with the above is the budget staffs' desire that factory people have more acquaintance with, and therefore respect for, the everyday problems of the finance staff in administering budgets.

4. Interestingly enough, most of the top controllers believed that the problems of administering the budget would not be alleviated until *finance people*, as well as factory people, changed. They felt that the budget people should be given a thorough course in self-understanding and in understanding and getting along with others—in other words, a course in human relations. For example:

> Yes, I feel education could do more. I think it should teach the person more about himself. I think there is altogether too much emphasis in human relations on understanding *others*. It seems to me that the first step toward understanding others is to understand yourself.

> I think a good accountant should get along with people. He can't be a "sour puss." I think he should be educated to understand people better. I think one of the important things that has been lacking is that accountants have never been trained to get their accounting figures across.

These, then, are the human problems involved in the administration of budgets and what can be done about them, as seen by the budget people.

8

Part III

WHAT FACTORY SUPERVISORS THINK OF BUDGETS

What Factory Supervisors Think Are:

- The Use of Budgets
- Budget Problems
- The Differences between Their Outlook and That of the Budget People
- Solutions to Some of these Problems

THE USE OF BUDGETS

Just how important are budgets and budget departments to factory supervisors? Each factory supervisor was asked to name the department which affected him the most and then the second most important. Fifty-seven percent considered production control as number one and forty-five percent chose the budget department as number one. Of the fifty-seven percent who picked the production control department as number one, *all* but one supervisor chose the budget department as the second most important department.

It seems relatively safe, therefore, to say that budgets wield an important influence in the production supervisor's world. Here are some typical comments:

> Well, if you want to study a department that has its clutches everywhere, go into the budget department. That's all over this plant.

> Costs are important here. They're the great godfathers of the company.

> Heck yes, by far, they make up a lot of trouble in the long run. But—well—er—they're not what they're cracked up to be.

In general, the supervisors close to the employees hardly ever used budgets. In fact, they suggested that the best way to cause trouble was to mention a budget directly or indirectly to the employees. The supervisors higher up in the line of authority did use them. Of course, their usage varied, but in general the budgets were used. We shall see subsequently that the amount of use by upper-level supervisors was closely related to the way they handled their subordinates.

Use by Front-Line Supervisors

In all the plants studied the research team obtained a definite impression that budgets were "taboo" with the employees who did the work. The writers could not help but sense an informal, but highly effective group norm of "no one speaks of or uses budgets seriously." This is, of course, merely an impression. No interviews were conducted with the employees to test the impression. Some idea of the validity of this observation may be obtained if one examines parts of the statements made below by the supervisors close to the people. These statements should also give the reader a vivid picture of the feelings and the human problems faced by these supervisors.

> I wish I were an accountant. I don't think a fellow should believe these figures until he sees five sets of them.

> I'm violently against the figures. I keep away from showing them to the workers. I *know my boys* are doing a good job. They're trying to do their best. If I give them the heat with this stuff they'll blow their top.

> You can't use budgets with the people. Just can't do anything like that. People have to be handled carefully and in our plant, carefully doesn't mean with budgets. Besides, I don't think *my* people are lazy.

> No, can't do it because some people see budgets as a target against a man. I'll have to admit that we cannot display the budget in front of our people. You have to be careful, you know. The first thing you know you'll have a grievance against you. We don't ask a man to look at a budget. Oh well, what we might do is put it under his nose so he can't help but see it. I should say, if we show the budget to any worker, it's only one out of every six.

> No, no, I couldn't even use a budget in front of my people. I just wouldn't dare. And, mind you, I *don't think* my top management would want us to. We wouldn't get any production out if we did.

> No sir, I can't use budgets to increase production. I don't dare go up and say to a man, "My budget is *up* $5,000 this year, John." He'd look at me in scorn. No sir, anything like that is using a *whip*. And the men *don't like it*.

> In fact, the best way to cause trouble is to bring that word into the picture.

Budgets, therefore, are far from being "cold pictures" of past production to the people. Rather they are symbols; symbols of something which may arouse fear, resentment, hostility, and aggression on the part of the employees toward the company and which may lead to decreased production.

The supervisor is, therefore, forced to refrain from mentioning budgets. He tries to accomplish what top management desires in distributing budget results, by translating these results into informal shop language and thereby calling these results to the attention of the employees. If he is not able to do this, he doesn't mention budgets at all.

The price for mentioning budgets is high. The supervisor who uses them explicitly is faced with a resentful work group which may express this resentment in many different ways, all of which lead to trouble for the supervisor.

It is not difficult, therefore, to see why a supervisor does not dare use budgets as some budget people want him to.

Use by Top-Factory Supervisors

We have seen that front-line supervisors are not able to use budgets freely with their employees. Top-factory supervisors, on the other hand, seem to use budgets quite frequently and strongly on the supervisors below them. In Part IV of this report this specific problem will be examined more closely and more analytically, but consider the following comments made by top-factory supervisors:

> Yes, I do discuss. We take a crack at the problem and see exactly why things are as they are. I'll go to my foreman and say, like I just did a few minutes ago, "Joe, now I expected a drop in production due to vacations, but look here, this is quite a drop." Now, I expect him to give me an answer.

> The job of budgets is to see to it that we *never forget* we've got a job to do. Sure, we apply pressure with budgets. I guess budgets aren't worth much unless they have a kick in them.

Clearly, the closer one is to the employees, the less one can use budgets to increase production or arouse interest in production. If such is the case, one begins to wonder about the supervisor who is in the position of receiving all the pressure from above, but cannot pass on the pressure to the people below him. Does all this pressure stay with the supervisor? This and other questions will be raised, and we hope partially answered, in Part IV.

What Factory Supervisors Think Are:

BUDGET PROBLEMS

Although there may be some differences among levels of supervision in the use of budgets, all the supervisors, regardless of their rank, were pretty much agreed concerning the limitations of budgets. Some of the limitations mentioned were:

Budget Reports only Include Results, not Reasons

Perhaps one of the greatest criticisms of budgets was the fact that they never included the reasons *why* they were not achieved by a certain supervisor. There was considerable feeling about this problem. Supervisors disliked intensely the fact that their departments would look "sick" on the budget while the reasons for the "sickness" were never published along with the results.

> Budgets never show the reasons *why* they have not been met. They never take into account all variables that affect production.

The budget might contain the finance man's explanation: e.g., "The reason 'why' this budget has not been met is excess labor costs, or too much waste of time getting the job ready to be produced, etc.", but such reasons were not the real explanations as seen by the supervisors. They wanted the budget to state *why* they had excess labor costs, or *why* it took too long to get the job ready.

In other words, the supervisor's *why* was never included. Only the *why* of the budget man was included. This *why* was on a completely different level from the factory supervisor's *why*. The budget man's *why* really states *what* trouble caused the budget not to be met, but it did not state why the trouble existed.

The comments of factory supervisors on this point are revealing:

> Let's say the budget tells me I was off. I didn't make it. That's of interest. But, it doesn't tell me the important thing of *why* I didn't make it, or how I am going to make it the next time. Oh sure, they might say all I need to do is increase production and cut out waste. Well, I know that. The question is *how* to do it.

> Budgets show a nice average for the month, quarter, or whatever it is. If I had 1,000 jobs in a month and I made my budget, that's fine. But, the fact that I made it doesn't describe how and what I had to do to make it. The budget never shows how I had to work, the headaches I had to surmount, especially with the bad jobs.

> I think the budget boys think things are simple—just add up the figures. But factory knows all the things that could easily affect them. These factors are important to us. There are so darn many extenuating circumstances about each budget. But the budget people just don't see these circumstances. 'Course we hardly tell them, because we had to do a little monkey business to come out right.

The following supervisor sheds additional light on the subject. It is interesting to note that he realizes why the budgets are not broken down further. But it is perhaps more interesting to note that even though he understands why budgets give only the total picture, he still feels quite strongly about them. Such data cannot help but lead one to wonder if a knowledge about budgets will really alleviate the feelings about them.

> As I see it, budgets are for top management. Top management is only interested in the total picture. They just want to see the results. They're just interested in knowing if the goal has been met.
>
> The deviations, the headaches are all ironed out for them at the end of the budget. *But, you can bet your boots,* they are *not* ironed out for me. They remain, to remind me of the many things that can go wrong in my department. It's like this: I'm in the forest. I see hundreds of different trees [problems] that go to make it up. Top management is up in the air looking down on the forest. They see a mass of green. Now the budget measures that mass of green, but they don't tell the top management anything about the different trees that make up the green. You might put it this way—my job is to worry about the *feelings* that go to make up these figures. Finance peoples' job is to worry about the figures without the emotions.

Emphasis on History

Another closely allied problem is that budgets emphasize *past performance.* Budgets are historical documents. As such, they are used primarily to project some predictions about the future based on the past.

Factory supervisors, on the other hand, place little emphasis on the past and hardly ever have time to think of the future. Their emphasis is on the *present* day-to-day situation. One supervisor expressed this as follows:

> The only thing I do know is that we should do the best job we can today. It's today, today, that is important. You can't think of tomorrow and tomorrow. It's today. Never mind years after. The fundamental results are what counts and the fundamental results occur today, not tomorrow.

Rigidity of Budgets

In addition to the emphasis on the past, supervisors felt there was an equally negative emphasis on *rigidity* of standards. Once established, budget people seemed to dislike changing standards. Most budget people, the factory supervisors stated, were inflexible.

This rigidity of the finance people, as seen by the factory supervisors, leads to some important feelings on the part of the latter. For example:

> I'd say one of the biggest problems is that budgets are set up on past performance. Once they come up with a figure, they hate to leave it. Two years ago, my budget on errors was 100, now it's 150, but our production has increased a lot more.
>
> Somehow the budget people freeze the figures in their minds and they just don't want to change.
>
> So, they set this budget up once and they hate to change. What happens? Easy—we have to figure our tricks. So we wait till it's time for the budget results to come out and we feed the machines all the easy orders we could keep around the shop so that we're sure we've made the budget.
>
> The finance people don't realize it, but all they do is process work and record what *has* been done. They're historians, that's all they are. If they could only realize that history isn't the whole picture.
>
> You know, if you really look at it, the factory supervisors are the real creators while the finance people create nothing. All they do is compute the results of the factory's work.

Budgets Apply Pressure for an Ever-Changing Goal

One of the more important criticisms the factory people had was the feeling that the people who set the budgets were never satisfied. For example:

> If I meet this budget, those guys up there will only raise it. Or, You can't let them know that you made the budget without too much trouble. If you do they'll up it as sure as hell.

These were typical remarks made by most of the factory supervisors. (In no case did the top-factory supervisor consider this to be a criticism.) It was quite obvious that the factory supervisors wondered when, if ever, the optimum level would be reached. For example:

> They make a budget and then constantly increase it. There's too much of that constant raising and raising that thing. Pretty soon the boys catch on and figure out it's the same old stuff. So they don't respond.
>
> Now, you tell me. Do they have to do that? They should set budgets fairly and keep them there. Then, if we're not meeting them, then we should sit down and analyze them. What is the sense of sitting down to analyze things when I know all they want to do is raise them?

The fact that budgets are used to increase production progressively has interesting results.

Budgets begin to be perceived as "perpetual needlers"; as top management "shots in the arm"; or as the "hammer that's waiting to hit you on the head."

The Implication that Budgets Motivate Supervisors to do a Better Job

As we have seen earlier, the finance people perceive budgets as goal-setters for factory supervisors. They feel that the supervisors are "kept on the ball" because of budgets. Some finance people suggest that factory supervisors would be "lost" without budgets. On the other hand, factory supervisors resent quite strongly being thought of as people who would lose their motivation if it were not for budgets.

Some of them agreed that budgets had a function of helping them accomplish their work, but few if any saw budgets as the creator of their motivation. To accept budgets as motivators is to imply that supervisors do not have adequate interest in their jobs. This is seen as an insult to a man's integrity and the factory supervisors resent it strongly. For example:

> I don't care much for budgets. I *can* use them, but I don't *need* them. My job is to get out the production, *and I do the best I know how*. What do I need budgets for? Now budgets can't help me in that.
>
> Budget! . Well, I know this is the way the other fellows feel about it. They *don't want to be bothered* with them. We do our job, and *we do the best job we can*. That's it. No matter what comes out, we know we've done our best.
>
> So you see, we work without budgets. We don't really need them.
>
> We don't need budgets to tell us to do a good job. Take an example: I have a poor man on machine A; I know we need a better man to get production out. So what do we do? I change him. Now, did I do that because I was thinking of budgets? No, it had nothing to do with that. I *was interested in doing a good job*. I was interested in getting production out.

Budgets Are Not Realistic

Another important criticism made by factory supervisors was that some budgets were purposely kept high so that they were almost impossible to meet. The supervisors definitely and sincerely resent this practice. They resent it primarily for two reasons:

Such a practice places a supervisor in a situation where he can never succeed. One supervisor expressed this when he said:

> There's not much sense in setting a budget that's too high. What good is it? If a man doesn't meet it, he's going to say, "to hell with it." It's going to get him to think they're never satisfied. If you ever want to discourage a guy, just give him a budget you know he can't meet.

Such a practice implies that the company does not believe the supervisor's own desire to do a good job is sufficient to meet reasonable budgets. The unrealistic budget is used to spur supervisors on, but it does not work and is resented. This was pointed out by a factory supervisor when he said:

> Budgets should be realistic. They should reflect the true picture. Take the error budget for example. There is something. The error figure is way too low. I know it. The people know it and so do the financial people know it.
>
> So I suggested to the financial people that they should increase it. They refused. They feel that if they increase the budget to a realistic level, and the people meet it, they'll have no reason to cut down errors.
>
> We, on the other hand, feel differently. Our people see the figure and they know it is ridiculously low. So they say, "Oh, those financial guys do that so they can have the opportunity to wave the flag."

The supervisors' comments certainly raise some question concerning the efficacy of setting budgets at an unreasonable level. This question, too, will be dealt with more fully later on.

What Factory Supervisors Think Are:

THE DIFFERENCES BETWEEN THEIR OUTLOOK AND THAT OF THE BUDGET PEOPLE

In Part II some differences in outlook between financial people and factory people as seen by the financial people were described. What are the differences in outlook as seen by the factory supervisors?

The first four basic differences as seen by the factory supervisors have already been discussed. They were:

1. Finance people are primarily interested in the past and the future. They don't think of the present.

2. Finance people tend to be too rigid once they have set up their figures.

3. Finance people see only the total picture. They never see the many problems that go to make up the total picture. They worry only about end results.

4. Finance people tend to see life only as a set of figures. They take the emotions out of life and deal only with the cold figures.

Some other differences have not been previously mentioned:

1. Finance people cannot see the other person's point of view. They know almost nothing about the problems a supervisor is faced with daily.

2. Finance people have a language of their own. It is completely different from the language of the shop.

3. The final difference is more in the area of attitudes. It was best expressed by one supervisor who said:

> A big problem with budget people, and all finance people for that matter, is that basically they are—well—let's see—yes—sarcastic.

> I think that they think they're the whole show. If you're asking for our opinions, we think they have an over-exalted opinion of their position.

What Factory Supervisors Think Are:

SOLUTIONS TO SOME OF THESE PROBLEMS

1. By far the most frequent and most stressed recommendation made by factory supervisors was that the finance people should learn to see the other person's point of view. The supervisors recommended that the finance people be given a "taste" of factory problems. Some typical comments were:

> They are not fully acquainted with our everyday production problems. They don't realize our troubles and our difficulties. The best thing to do is to bring them down and see our problems.

> I'd tell you what I'd teach them: to know my job. See the problems I have. Bring them down here and see what *really goes on*.

2. The financial people should undergo some training to learn that budgets are not final. They are merely opinions. One supervisor stated:

> Yes, I could recommend a good thing. I wish they could have their thinking about budgets changed. They are too rigid. Budgets are statements of *opinions* not *facts*. That's their big trouble. They think budgets are facts.

3. The financial people should change their belief that the employee is lazy and wants to do as little work as possible. For example:

> I'd like to see them change their attitude that employees are out to get them [budget people] and do as little work as they can get away with.

4. Closely related to recommendation (3) above is one that recurred often: finance people should change their belief that the best way to raise production is through pressure.

5. Financial people should be taught that they are not superior to factory supervisors. Some typical comments:

> I'd deflate their ego—I'd give them something to take them down a peg.

> I'd like to teach them not to think their budgets are too important.

Part IV

AN ANALYSIS OF THE IMPACT OF BUDGETS ON PEOPLE

- The Problem of Pressure:
  - The Causes of Pressure
  - The Effects of Pressure
  - The Creation of Groups
  - Pressure on Front-Line Supervisors
- Success for Budget Supervisors Means Failure for Factory Supervisors:
  - Reporting Shortcomings of the Foreman
  - Effects of Failure on People
  - The Wall between Finance and Factory People
- The Problem of Department-Centered Supervisors:
  - What Makes an Organization
  - Controlling Conflicts Among Departments
- Budgets as a Medium for Personality Expression
- The Human Problems of Budgets — A Case Example
- Summary

It is difficult to differentiate sharply between description and analysis. Some problems involved in budgeting have been analyzed already in the preceding descriptive chapters. This part of the report, however, is devoted entirely to an analysis of some of the most crucial problems that arise from, or are related to, budgeting in an organization.

THE PROBLEM OF PRESSURE

One of the most common of the factory supervisors' attitudes about budgets was that budgets were used as a pressure device to increase production efficiency. Many cases were cited to support this point. Finance people also admitted that budgets helped "keep people on the ball" by raising their goals and increasing their motivation. The problem of the effects of pressure applied through budgets seems to be the core of the budget problem.

The Causes of Pressure

Employees and front-line supervisors believe that the cause for pressure from the top is due to top management's belief that most employees are basically or inherently lazy. Employees and front-line supervisors also feel that top management believes that employees do not have enough motivation of their own to do the best possible job.

The interviews with top management officials revealed that the employees' beliefs were not totally unfounded, as a few quotations from some of the top management (both line and finance) make clear:

> I'll tell you my honest opinion. Five per cent of the people work, ten per cent of the people think they work. And the other eighty-five per cent would rather die than work.

> I think there is a need for more pressure. People need to be needled a bit. I think man is inherently lazy and if we could only increase the pressure, I think the budget system would be more effective.

> There are lots of workers in the plant, hundreds of them, who don't have any more capacity to do things other than what they're doing. And they're *lazy!* They might be able to develop some capacities, and I think there's a lot of them even in their desire to do so couldn't do it, even if they want to. But, *they don't even have the desire.*

Such feelings, even if they are never overtly expressed toward employees, filter through to the employees in very subtle ways. Budgets represent one of these more subtle ways. Once the employees sense these feelings exist in top managment, they may become very resentful. Some supervisors expressed a warning concerning these feelings as follows:

> They [*employees*] have an established concept of a fair output. Now, if you believe, like most financial people do, that the average worker is out to cheat the company all the time, I give up.

> They [*top finance and factory*] ought to change their attitudes that employees are out to get them.

> Well, I guess they think we need this needling. But *I don't think so.*

The Effects of Pressure

How do people react to pressure? In three of the plants studied factory supervisors felt they were working under pressure and that the budget was the principal instrument of pressure. Management exerts pressure on the work force in many ways, of which budgets is but one. Budgets, being concrete, seem to serve as a medium through which the total effects of management pressure are best expressed. As such they become an excellent point of focus for studying the effect of pressure on people in a working organization.

An example may help point up what happens when management "puts on the pressure." The work force of a plant is producing at 70% of its efficiency.[1] Since the level of efficiency is 70% there must be (1) certain forces which keep it from falling below 70% and (2) certain forces which prevent it from going above 70%.

What are some of the forces which keep it from falling below 70%?

- Budget talks to foremen
- Red circling of poor showing of the departments in the budget results
- Production drives
- Pep talks by supervisors using budgets as evidence
- Threat of reprimand if budget is not met
- Threat of feeling of failure if budget is not met

---

[1] For the sake of illustration, assume that the technical efficiency of the plant is at a maximum and that human efficiency, or effort, has to be increased if production is to be raised.

What are some of the forces which prevent efficiency from going above 70%?

- Informal agreements among employees not to produce more
- Fear of loss of job if efficiency increases
- Formal (union) agreements against "speedups"
- Abilities of individual employees
- Abilities of work teams as a whole

In our example the level of production is stable, therefore both sets of force are equal in strength. Suppose that top management decides to increase production. Usually, thought is immediately given to adding more factors to those that help increase production. The logic is that if these forces can be strengthened, they overcome the forces which tend to prevent efficiency from rising and thereby increase production.

Budgets are but one part, but an important one, in this new "push." Finance people are usually asked to scrutinize all budgets carefully. They are directed to cut out all "the lace and niceties" and "get down to essentials." In short, a new pressure upwards is expressed somewhere in the new budgets in terms of a new, "tighter" figure.

The results may be as expected. Human efficiency rises, for example, 10%, and production is increased. A new level of efficiency is stabilized at 80%.

But, actually something else has occurred concurrently with this new push which management may not perceive. Since the level of human efficiency was stabilized at 80%, presumably factors that keep production down *also increased* until they equaled the factors that tend to increase production. Therefore, coupled with an increase in production, the plant also acquires an increase in forces directed in the opposite direction. People and groups are now working harder to keep production at this new level and prevent it from rising again. It is not difficult to see what happens. Tension begins to mount. People become uneasy and suspicious. They increase the informal pressure to keep production at the new level. Any new increase will have to be "paid for" by management (e.g., "free" tickets to football games, slowdowns, strikes, etc.).

Moreover, management has to work harder to keep the new strength of the forces, which tend to drag down efficiency, from overwhelming the forces which resulted in increased production. They will find themselves constantly looking for new ideas, new methods to keep the production at the present level. Any slight decrease in pressure on their part will result in an immediate slowdown.

Finally, this constant increasing pressure from top management for greater production may lead to long-term negative results. People living under these conditions tend to become suspicious of every new move management makes to increase production. Budgets seem to become one of the targets for resentment since they are one of the techniques most frequently used by management to increase the pressure for higher production.

The Creation of Groups

An increase in tension, resentment, suspicion, fear and mistrust may not be the only result of ever stronger management pressures transmitted to supervisors, and in turn, to employees. We know, from psychological research, that people can stand a certain amount of pressure. After this point is passed, it becomes intolerable to an individual. We also know that one method people have to reduce the effect of the pressure (assuming that the employees cannot reduce the pressure itself) is to join groups. These groups then help absorb much of the pressure and the individual is personally relieved.

The process of individuals joining groups to relieve themselves of pressure is not an easy one. It does not occur overnight. The development of a group on such a basis seems to have the following general stages of growth:

First, the individuals "feel" the pressure. They are not certain, but they sense an increase in pressure.

Second, they begin to see definite evidences of the pressure. They not only feel it, they can point to it.

Since they feel this pressure is on them personally, they begin to experience tension and general uneasiness.

Next, the people usually "feel out" their fellow workers to see if they sense the pressure.

Finding out that others have noted the pressure, the people begin to feel more at ease. It helps to be able to say, "I'm not the only one."

Finally, they realize that they can acquire emotional support from each other by becoming a group. Furthermore, they can "blow their top" about this pressure in front of their group. Gradually therefore, the individuals become a group because in becoming a group they are able to satisfy these needs:

1. A need to reduce the pressure on each individual

2. A need to get rid of tension

3. A need to feel more secure by belonging to a group which can counteract the pressure

In short, a new, cohesive group has developed to *combat* management pressure. In a sense, the people have learned that they can be happier if they combine *against* this management pressure.

Suppose now that top management, aware of the tensions which have been generated and the groups which have been formed, seeks to reduce the pressure. The emphasis on budgets is relaxed. Perhaps even the standards are "loosened." Does this then destroy the group? After all, it's primary reason for existence was to combat the pressure. Now, the pressure is gone. The group should eventually disintegrate.

The answer seems to be that the group continues to exist!

The evidence for this is not as conclusive as it should be. Therefore, the following explanation should be considered primarily in the realm of inference and conjecture rather than scientific fact.

These factors seem to operate to keep the group in existence:

1. There is a "time lag" between the moment management announced the new policy and the time the workers put it into effect.

2. The individuals have made a new and satisfactory adjustment with each other. They have helped to satisfy each other's needs. They are, as the social scientist would say, "in equilibrium" with each other. Any attempt to destroy this balance will tend to be resisted even if the attempt represents an elimination of a "bad" or unhealthy set of conditions. People have *created* a stable pattern of life and they will resist a change in this pattern.

3. The individuals fear pressure will come again in the future. Because of this feeling, they will tend to create unreal conditions or to exaggerate existing conditions so that they can rationalize to themselves that pressure still exists and, therefore, the need for the group also exists.

In the course of this study, for instance, employees were interviewed who admitted management had officially announced a new policy of less pressure and more participation. But, at the same time, they expressed suspicion about the participation and suggested it was a new way to cover up the old pressure. Others admitted freely that they passed on unverified rumors about management intentions. In short, the people were doing their best to create conditions, *in their minds*, that would permit them to feel the pressure was still present, and therefore, the need for the group was still strong.

Pressure on Front-Line Supervisors

But what about the foreman? Strong pressures converge upon him. How does he protect himself from these pressures?

He cannot join a group against management, as his work force does. For one reason, he probably has at least partially identified himself with management. For another reason, he may be trying to advance in the hierarchy. Naturally, he would not help his chances for advancement if he joined a group against management.

The evidence of the previous chapters seems to indicate that the line supervisor cannot pass all the pressure he receives to his employees. Time and time again the factory supervisors stated that passing the pressure down would only create conflict and trouble which would lead to a decrease in production.

The question arises, where does the pressure go? How do the supervisors relieve themselves of at least some of the pressure? There is evidence to suggest at least three ways in which pressure is handled by the supervisors:

1. Interdepartmental strife. The foremen release some of the pressure by continuously trying to blame fellow foremen for the troubles that exist. "They are," as one foreman expressed it, "trying to throw the dead cat in each other's backyard."

In three plants observed, much time was spent by certain factory supervisors in trying to lay the blame for errors and problems on some other department.

2. Staff *versus* factory strife. The foremen released much of the pressure by blaming the budget people, production control people and salesmen for their problems. The data already presented concerning factory supervisors' attitudes towards budget people substantiate this point.

3. "Internalizing" pressure. Many supervisors who do not express their feelings about the pressure have in reality "internalized" it and, in a sense, made it a part of themselves. Such damming up of pressure seemed to be expressed in the following ways:

(i) Supervisor A is quiet, relatively nonemotional, seldom expresses his negative feelings to anyone, but at the same time he works excessively. Supervisor A can be found working at his desk long after the others have gone home. As one supervisor expressed it, "That guy works himself to death."

(ii) Supervisor B is nervous, always running around "checking up" on all his employees. He usually talks fast, gives one the impression that he is "selling" himself and his job when interviewed. He is forever picking up the phone, barking commands and requesting prompt action.

Both of these types (or a combination of these types) are expressions of much tension and pent up emotions that have been internalized. People working under such conditions finally are forced to "take it easy," or they find themselves with ulcers or a nervous breakdown.

But that is not the end of the problem. Constant tension leads to frustration. A frustrated person no longer operates as effectively as he was accustomed. He finds that he tends to forget things he used to remember. Work that he used to do with pleasure, he now delegates to someone else. He is no longer able to make decisions as fast as he did months ago. Now he finds he has to take a walk or get a cup of coffee—anything to get "away from it all."

Putting on the Pressure When Business Falls Off

Most finance people agreed that budgets were used with greatest force when times were bad. As soon as sales and profits decreased and the economic future began to look black, then budgets were emphasized and strengthened.

The foreman, who is already living in a pressure-laden and tension-full world, suddenly finds himself (with others) in a bad economic period. All the stresses and strains, both at home and in the plant, which are associated with poor economic conditions are added to the already existing tension-creating factors in his life. But, to make matters worse, management usually adds a third set of factors which increases this tension by applying all sorts of pressure, through budgeting, upon the supervisor.

The results are immediately evident. Extreme work, or extreme aggression become "natural"—part of "human nature" of the supervisor. Such stress will result in the supervisor's attempt to alleviate some of the factors causing the tension. This may lead to quick or ill-conceived or confused or violent action on the part of the supervisor.[2]

Withdrawal, apathy, and indifference may result in order that the supervisor can protect himself from the stress and strains. Rumors become more evident. Mistrust, suspicion, and a lack of tolerance increase. In short, conflict, tension, and unhappiness become the key characteristics of the supervisor's life.

In summary, then, in order to increase human efficiency from 70% to 80%, pressure was applied through the medium of the budget. Adding to the forces which increase efficiency

[2] Alexander Leighton, *The Governing of Men.* (Princeton University Press, 1946.) See especially the Appendices.

also strengthened the forces which decrease efficiency. Employees sought to relieve themselves of increased tension by combining into groups. Front-line supervisors, prevented from grouping, either "took it out" on other foremen or on the budget people, or else bottled it up within themselves. It seems possible that in this example management has mortgaged the future to bring about an immediate increase in efficiency.

The necessity for constantly increasing efficiency is, however, a basic fact of life in business. If increasing efficiency generates forces which in the long run decrease efficiency, what is the answer? The answer may well lie in the area of concentrating on decreasing those forces which tend to decrease efficiency, rather than increasing the forces which tend to increase efficiency. Some of the possibilities will be examined in Part V of this report.

Success for Budget Supervisors Means Failure for Factory Supervisors

Students of human relations agree that most people want to feel successful. We observe people constantly defining social and psychological goals, struggling to meet them, and as they are met, feeling successful.

Finance and factory supervisors are no exception. The typical finance supervisor does his work as best he can. He hopes and expects just praise of this work from *his superior*. Most of his success comes, therefore, from his superior's evaluation. It is the "boss" who will eventually say "well done", or recommend a promotion. In other words, a finance supervisor measures his success on his job, to a substantial degree, by the reactions of his superior.

The situation is the same for the factory supervisor. He also desires success. Like the finance supervisor, much of his success also derives from the comments and behavior the "boss" exhibits. In short, the factory supervisor is also oriented toward the top for an evaluation of how well he is doing his job.

What is the task of a good and successful finance supervisor? The reader will recall that the finance people perceive their task as being the watchdog of the company. They are always trying to improve the situation in the plant. As one finance supervisor said, "*Always*, there is room to make it better." And finally, the reader will recall the statement that, "The budget man has made an excellent contribution to this plant. He's found a lot of things that were *sour*. You might say a good budget man . . . lets top management know if anything is *wrong*."

In other words, their success derives from finding errors, weaknesses, and faults that exist in the plant. But, when they discover these errors, weaknesses, and faults, they also single out a "guilty party" and implicitly, at least, accuse him of failure. This is true because in finding weaknesses, errors or faults in a certain department, one is at the same time telling the factory supervisors that "things aren't going along as well as they could be." This, naturally, gives many factory supervisors a feeling of failure.

To be sure, such an occurrence will not make every supervisor feel he has failed. Some supervisors do not worry much about their job. Therefore, we find that the *supervisor who really feels the failure is the one who is highly interested in doing a good job.*

Reporting Shortcomings of the Foreman

The way in which these shortcomings are reported is also important:

Assume that finance man A discovers an error in foreman B's department. How is this error reported? Does the finance man go directly to the factory foreman? In the plants studied the answer, usually, is "no."

The finance man cannot take the "shortest" route between the foreman and himself. For one reason, it may be a violation of policy for a staff man to go directly to a line man. But, more important (from a human point of view), the staff man derives his success when *his boss knows* he is finding errors. Therefore, his boss would never know how good a job finance man A is doing unless it came to his attention. In short, perhaps because of organizational regulations but basically because much success in industry is derived from above, the finance person usually takes his findings to his own boss, who in turn gives it to his, and so on up the line and across and down into the factory line structure.

Taking the long way around has at least one more positive value for finance people. The middle and top management finance people also derive some success in being able to go to the plant manager and point to some newly discovered weaknesses in the factory. Therefore, not only one man obtains feelings of success, but all interested people up the entire finance structure obtain some feeling of satisfaction.

But, how about the factory people? The answer seems evident. They experience a certain sense of "being caught with their pants down." Foreman B is really placed in a failure situation. He not only experiences the negative feelings of being wrong, but also the negative feelings of knowing that his superiors know it, and that he has placed them in an undesirable situation. Therefore, while the finance man A obtained a multiple dose of success, the factory foreman B obtained a multiple dose of failure.

Finally, to add insult to injury, the entire incident is made permanent and exhibited to the plant officials by being placed in some budget report which is to be, or has been, circulated through many top channels.

Effects of Failure on People

One might ask: What effects does this kind of failure have upon an individual? If they were insignificant, obviously we would not be concerned. Such is not the case. Feelings of failure can have devastating effects upon an individual, his work and his relationships with others.

Lippitt and Bradford, reporting on some ingenious scientific experiments conducted on the subject of success and failure, state that people who fail tend to:

- Lose interest in their work
- Lower their standards of achievement
- Lose confidence in themselves
- Give up quickly
- Fear any new task and refuse to try new methods or accept new jobs
- Expect failure
- Escape from failure by daydreaming
- Increase their difficulty in working with others
- Develop a tendency to blame others, to be over-critical of others' work and to develop trouble with other employees

On the other hand, people who succeed tend to:

- Raise their goals
- Gain greater interest in the activity in which they are engaged
- Gain greater confidence in their ability in the activity
- Increase their persistence to future goals
- Increase their ability to cooperate and work
- Increase their ability to adapt readily to new situations
- Increase their emotional control

In summary, we should point out that finance people aren't inherently "out to get them" as factory people in the plants described them. Rather, they are placed in a social organization where the only way in which they can receive success is to place someone else in failure.

The Wall Between Finance and Factory People

At least two more very interesting conditions are related to this peculiar position which the finance people hold:

First, since the budget people are always looking for weaknesses, errors, and faults, they begin to develop a philosophy of life in which their symbol for success is, not only the error discovered, but the very *thought* of the discovery of a possible *new* error. "Weaknesses," "discovery of errors made by others"—which are symbols of failure for others—are symbols of success for the budget people.

The realization and admission by budget people of the peculiar position in which they are placed, leads to the second interesting condition. The budget people tend to become defensive about their work. They don't like placing people in failure, but they have to. Being aware of this difficulty and the negative feelings it may create, they tend to become defensive about queries concerning "their books" or their methods. One has the feeling that, at times, they use their technical "know-how" and language to confuse the factory people. This confusion of the factory people serves, of course, as a defense for the budget man. As one man suggested, "After all, if they don't know anything about budgets, how can they criticize them"? In short, the ignorance of the factory people concerning budgets may become a wall behind which the finance people may work unmolested. It is interesting to note that one of the major causes of insecurity among factory supervisors concerning budgets (i.e., "we can't understand them") is one of the primary factors of security for the budget people.

There seems little doubt that the problem of success and failure is a major one. It needs further study. The present research has merely identified it.

The Problem of Department-Centered Supervisors

We have already shown that supervisors are partially evaluated by budget records. The factory supervisor, who desires to be known as being an efficient, effective supervisor, must make certain that his daily, weekly, monthly, and quarterly results compare favorably with the predicted results defined by the budgets. In short, a factory supervisor will feel successful, other things being equal, when he "meets his budget."

The phrase "meets his budget" is crucial. The budgets, which measure the effectiveness of a supervisor, continually emphasize to each supervisor the importance of *his*, and *primarily* his, department. The budget records he receives show *his* department's mistakes, *his* department's errors, *his* department's production. The accent is on his department. In other words, the budgets emphasize that the supervisor should constantly examine his department as *against* the other departments.

The interviews with the factory supervisors left little doubt that they were department-centered in outlook, rather than plant-centered. For example:

> The other day, I received an order to do a job, but no requisition. I called up production control and asked what was going on. I said to them, "Why didn't I get the requisition on that order?" They started to give excuses. Sure, they didn't worry. *This was my job, just like I don't have to worry when the other departments stand still.*

> No, each one of us gets his *own* picture when we get the budget results. Even if we got the total picture, it wouldn't mean much to us. We go right for our sheet. . . . As I said, we might get the whole plant picture, *but we're primarily interested in our own department.*

> No, I don't get a picture of the other people's budgets in this place and I don't think I need one or even want one. My main responsibility is in this here outfit of mine. *Nowhere else.* So, let them worry about their problem and I'll worry about mine.

The basis for a philosophy which budgets emphasize may be expressed as follows: "If every supervisor worries about his own department, there will be no trouble in the plant." Therefore, if each supervisor is made primarily responsible for the production picture of his part of the whole picture, no problems will arise.

Such a philosophy overlooks an extremely important point, perhaps described by the statement, "An organization is something different from the sum of the individual parts." The difference of the whole from the sum of the parts lies in the fact that the parts of an organization exist in certain *relationships* with each other. It is these relationships which create the difference.

What Makes an Organization

Parts, alone, do not make a whole organization. One cannot conceive of "adding" parts of an organization any more than adding together the hundreds of pieces that make up a watch in order to make the watch run. The crucial problem is to place the parts in correct relationship to each other.

Without laboring the point it seems clear that important relationships between departments are disregarded by an overemphasis on the individual departments. If everyone made certain his own department was functioning correctly, but at the same time, did not pay attention to the functioning of his department in relation to others, then trouble would still arise.

Such, in fact, occurs in those plants which make forceful use of budgets. The supervisors think only of their own departments. Few, if any, worry about the relationships between departments. The inevitable soon occurs. As soon as a mistake is uncovered or an important error is made, the supervisors try to blame someone else and/or make certain their department is not the one to be penalized.

Controlling Conflicts Among Departments

It might be suggested that the control of the relationships between departments rests with the plant manager, or some higher authority. From his high position, he is best able to control the conflict between departments. The crux of the matter is that this is all the leader can do, i.e., *control* conflict. He is unable to eliminate it since the causes for the conflict are not within his reach. Since the top leader controls this conflict, the supervisors increasingly look to the leader to "break up a fight" or settle a dispute. This forces the supervisors to become increasingly dependent upon the leader. Furthermore, the more successful the top leader is, the less the supervisors need to worry about cooperation. They soon learn that the leader will solve any inter-departmental problems.

An example will illustrate the point.

In one of the plants studied a mistake was made on a customer order. The customer sent the material back to the plant. The error was corrected and the material sent back to the customer.

The cost of making the correction was nearly three thousand dollars. The error, especially since it was so large, had to be entered in the budget records. Some department had to be charged with the error. The problem was, who should be charged with the error?

For two months, supervisors of the departments most likely to be blamed waged a continuous campaign to prove their innocence. Each supervisor blamed the others. No one wanted the error on his record. The supervisors actually spent hundreds of man-hours arguing and debating among themselves. Emotions were aroused, people began calling each other names. Finally, two of the supervisors refused to talk to each other. Conflict reigned among the supervisors.

But, the supervisors were not the only persons in conflict. The division manager was also in conflict. He had to make the decision. To charge any supervisor with such an error would certainly invite hostility from that supervisor. This hostility might have further effects in the future. The division manager did not want to risk a weakening of his relationship, especially with a supervisor. But, he had to make a decision.

A meeting was held with the interested supervisors. The problem was discussed until just about everybody and everything that could be blamed, were blamed for the error. The division manager finally "gave in." He decided to place the error under "general factory loss." No department would be affected. The plant, as a whole, would carry the stigma. The division manager expressed his thoughts behind his decision to the research worker as follows:

> Take that big three thousand dollar error. We have to charge it up to someone. One man blames sales, another someone else. Everyone refuses to admit it might be their own fault. They each blame someone else.
>
> Well, I don't know. Perhaps, I thought it might be best to put the whole thing under general factory loss. Or else, they'd be hurt.

Note that the supervisors are willing to have the *plant* as a whole take the blame. But, they resist any attempts to place the blame on their individual departments.

In summary, budgets and budgeting tend to make the supervisor think of *his*, and essentially only his, department. Budget records, as administered, foster a narrow viewpoint on the part of the user. The budget records serve as a constant reminder that the important aspect to consider is one's own department and *not* one's own plant. As a result, supervisors become department centered rather than plant centered.[3]

Budgets as a Medium for Personality Expression

The final problem to be discussed became evident only after a series of interviews with different controllers and top factory officials.

[3] One method to remedy this problem is to attempt to have the staff person report directly to the factory. For an interesting statement of this case see: Douglas MacGregor, "The Role of the Human Relations Consultant," *Journal for the Study of Social Issues*, Vol. IV, Summer 1948.

Then it became obvious that the way people expressed their interest in budgets, and the way in which they described and used them, were directly related to the pattern of leadership they used in their daily industrial life.

For example, if a rather domineering, aggressive, "go-getting" top executive was interviewed, his presentation of the problem would also be made in a domineering, aggressive, "go-getting" manner. Therefore, although it is accurate to state that budgets are composed of "cold, nonhuman symbols" (i.e., figures), it is equally valid to state that once human beings use these "nonhuman figures," they project onto these figures all the emotions and feelings at their command.

An incident which occurred in one of the plants studied may illustrate this point. At the close of a particularly violent budget meeting in which a top executive flayed his subordinates, he ended by saying, "Now, fellows, I'm sorry I got hot. But it's these darn budget figures—well you know, I worry about them."

The subordinates all nodded their heads that they understood. The subordinates left the meeting room feeling, "Those darn budgets again. They *got the boss all upset.*"

This feeling (that the budgets caused the boss to be upset), although highly prevalent when such instances occur, is not at all accurate. It was *not* the budgets that "got the boss all upset." The budgets were merely a medium through which the boss could *express* the fact that he was upset. Obviously, budgets *per se* can do nothing. It is the people who use them that *cause* the behavior observed. Budgets, then, can be used to express one's pattern of leadership.

Because budgets become a medium of personality and leadership expression, and since people's personalities and leadership patterns are different, this research study found a number of methods with which top factory executives used budgets. A few of these methods are illustrated by the following comments made by top factory supervisors:

> I go to the office and check that budget every day. I can then see how we're meeting the budget. If it's O.K., I don't say anything. But, if it's no good, then I come back here [*smiles*] and give the boys a little . . . Well, you know. I needle them a bit. I give them the old . . . hm . . . well . . . you know what . . . the old needle.

> I make it a policy to have close contact, human contact, with all the people in my department.
> If I see we're not hitting the budget, I go out and tell them I have $40,000 on the order.
> Well, they don't know what that $40,000 means. They think it's a lot of money so they get to work.
> Human factor, that's important. If you treat a human being like a human being, you can use them better and get more out of them.

> You know it's a funny thing. If I want my people to read the budget, I don't shove it under their nose. I just lay it on my desk and leave it alone. They'll pick it up without a doubt.

It is hoped that the above descriptions are adequate to convey the point that budgets furnish a means of expression. They serve to permit the user's pattern of leadership to blossom forth.

The Human Problems of Budgets—A Case Example

This section describes a meeting called by a top factory executive to discuss the problems of waste in his organization, especially the waste in two departments. The incident has been chosen not only because it portrays how budgets are used as media through which the factory executive expresses his personality, but because it describes the problems of department centeredness of supervisors as a result of the pressure previously discussed.

Present at the meeting were the supervisors of the two departments, two budget people, the supervisors of the department that supplies the material, and the top executive whom we shall call the leader.

> Leader: I've called you fellows down to get some ideas about this waste. I *can't* see why we're having so much waste. I just can't see it.
> Now [*turns to one of the supervisors*], I've called in these two budget men to get some ideas about this waste. Maybe they can give us an idea of how much some of the arguments you're going to give are worth.

> Cost man 1 to Leader: [*Slightly red—seems to realize he is putting the supervisors "on the spot".*] Well, er—we might be wrong, but I can't see how. There's an entire .1% difference and that's a lot.

> Supervisor A to Supervisor B: [*Trying to see if he could place the blame on Supervisor B.*] Well, maybe—maybe—some of your boys are throwing away the extra material I sent back to your department.

Supervisor B: [*Becomes red, answers quickly and curtly.*] No, no. We're re-working the extra material and getting it ready to use over again.

Supervisor A: [*Realizing that that argument wasn't going to hold much water.*] Well—you know—I've been thinking, maybe it's those new trainees we have in the plant. Maybe they're the cause for all the waste.

Leader: I can't understand that. Look here—look at their budget, their [*trainees'*] waste is low.

The meeting continued for another twenty minutes. It was primarily concerned with the efforts of Supervisors A and B to fix the blame on someone except themselves. The leader terminated the meeting as follows:

Leader: All right, look here, let's get busy on this—all of you—all of *us*, let's do something about it.

Supervisor B left the meeting, flushed, tense, and obviously unhappy. As he passed through the door, he muttered to himself, "Those g—d—budgets!" [*Note that the budgets are immediately blamed for the unhappiness.*]

Supervisor B hurried down to his area of the plant. He rushed in the office and called his subordinates abruptly—e.g., "Joe—get over here—I want to speak to you—something up."

The subordinates came in, all wondering what had occurred. As soon as they had all assembled, the supervisor started:

Supervisor B: Look, we've just *got* to get at this waste. It makes me look like—. Now let's put our heads together and "get on the ball".

The subordinates set to work to locate the causes for the waste. Their methods were interesting. Each one of them *first* checked to see, as one of them put it, "that the other guys [*departments*] aren't cheating us." A confidential statement finally arrived in Supervisor B's hands from one of the subordinates to the effect that he had located the cause for waste in another department.

Supervisor B became elated, but at the same time was angry at the fact that he had been made to look "sick" at the meeting with the leader.

Supervisor B: . . . I'm going to find out why they are making the waste. I don't mind taking a little—, as long as it's me that's doing the trouble.

Supervisor B roared out of his office and headed straight for the office of Supervisor A, where the confidential sources had reported the waste. Supervisor A saw him coming, and braced himself for the onslaught.

Supervisor B: —, I found out that it's your boys causing the waste. —, I want to know why— . . .

Supervisor A: [*Cuts Supervisor B off . . . spits out some tobacco and says—*] Now, you just hold on to your water. Don't get your blood up. I'll tell you. . . .

Briefly, we have tried to show by a running account of one small problem, the effects budgets can have upon people. In this cost-conscious plant, five or six people on the supervisory level spent many man-hours trying to place the blame on someone else.

SUMMARY

This exploratory research has led to the tentative conclusion that budgets and budgeting can be related to at least four important human relations problems:

First, budget pressure tends to unite the employees against management, and tends to place the factory supervisor under tension. This tension may lead to inefficiency, aggression, and perhaps a complete breakdown on the part of the supervisor.

Second, the finance staff can obtain feelings of success only by finding fault with factory people. These feelings of failure among factory supervisors lead to many human relations problems.

Third, the use of budgets as "needlers" by top management tends to make the factory supervisors see only the problems of their own department. The supervisors are not concerned with the other people's problems. They are not "plant-centered" in outlook.

Finally, supervisors use budgets as a way of expressing their own patterns of leadership. When these patterns result in people getting hurt, the budget, in itself a neutral thing, often gets blamed.

THE OBSERVATIONS AND ANALYSES contained on the preceding pages are decidedly exploratory. Before any specific recommendations can be made considerably more research must take place in this area. We are all well aware that the study of human relations is in its infancy, but it is a healthy, lusty infant with tremendous promise for the future.

As was pointed out in the introduction, if the observations made in this study lead the reader to think about the impact of budgets on people in his organization, then the purpose of this study will be accomplished. Most Foundation studies have been aimed at learning from the experience of others; the objective of this study is to spark the reader to learn more about himself and his own budget problems.

To provide more "food for thought" the Foundation Staff asked the research group to suggest avenues of approach to some of the problems uncovered by this report. The following pages contain their suggestions. These suggestions are not recommendations in the sense that they result from a full-blown, complete study of the problems of budgeting. They obviously do not. They are, however, drawn in part from the observations of this study, in part from results of a large number of studies in the human relations field, and in part from the personal experience, and therefore, the personal opinions, of the research group.

The following pages contain additional thought provokers.

Part V

SUGGESTIONS FOR ACTION

- Participation in the Budget Process
- Obtaining Acceptance of Budget Changes
- Obtaining Acceptance at the Supervisors' Meeting
- Training in Human Relations:
  - in the Schools
  - in Industry
- Suggestions for Further Research

In the preceding pages we have discussed our observations and findings in an extremely complex field—the impact of budgets upon people. Because problems are so complex and our research so obviously exploratory, we undertake the task of suggesting lines of action with considerable humility.

There are two areas in which action may prove fruitful. The first is the problem of getting participation for and an acceptance of budgets or budget changes. Interviews with controllers suggest that this area is a crucial one. Time and time again, the research group was told that the best way to gain acceptance is to have the supervisors participate in the making or the changing of budgets that affect them. The record area in which suggestions for action may be helpful is that of training in human relations. All the controllers interviewed were well aware of the need for broadening the normally "figure-conscious" budget man.

Participation in the Budget Process

The controller in a highly budget-conscious plant constantly evaluates, examines, and changes, if necessary, his budget control. These changes are usually made after many months of careful, detailed, and rigorous study. No changes are recommended unless the controller is certain they are needed and until all the "bugs" of the new system have been ironed out. Once the new changes are ready, the interested supervisors (both line and staff) are called in for a complete and honest discussion. All the controllers emphasized the need for *participation* of all key people in instituting any changes.

The insistence on participation sounded good to the research staff. But, after a few minutes of discussion, we began to wonder if the word "participation" had the same meaning for each of us. One thing, in particular, happened in every interview which led us to believe that we were not thinking of the same thing. After the controller had told us that he insisted on participation, he would then continue by describing to us the difficulty he has in getting the supervisors to speak freely. "We bring them in, we *tell* them that we want their frank opinion, but most of them just sit there and nod their heads. We know they're not coming out with exactly how they feel. I guess budgets scare them . . . . some of them don't have too much education . . . ." And still later, most controllers usually added, "Then we request the line supervisor to sign the new budget. Then he can't tell us he didn't accept it. We've found a signature helps an awful lot. If anything goes wrong, they can't come to us, as they often do, and complain. We just show them their signature and remind them they were shown exactly what the budget was made up of . . . ."

Such statements seem to indicate "pseudo-participation." That is, participation which looks like, but is not, real participation. True participation means that the people can be observed to be spontaneous and free in their discussion. Participation, in the real sense of the word, also involves a group decision which leads the group to accept or reject something new. Of course, organizations need to have their supervisors accept the new goals, not reject them, but if the supervisors do not really accept the new changes, but say they do, then trouble will exist. Such an acceptance is characterized by the necessity of the person who induced the change to be always on the "look out," to request signatures of the "acceptors" so that they cannot deny they "accepted," should they later complain, and to constantly apply pressure (through informal talks, meetings, and "educational discussions of accounting") upon the "acceptors."

In other words, if top management executives are going to use participation, then it should be used in the real sense of the word. Any dilution of the real stuff "will taste funny" and people will not like it.

Perhaps true participation cannot be obtained for certain decisions, but can be obtained for other decisions. We feel that in the typical plant most of the over-all goals of a plant or even a department cannot be set by the members of the plant or the department. But, the path by which these goals are to be met, the way these goals are to be accomplished, can be decided upon cooperatively by the interested employees. In other words, if top management has set down a profit goal for the year, then there is not much sense in saying the people participated in setting that goal. Nor, should management try to get them to feel this is *their* goal (in the sense that they created it). It is not. But top management may try to make them feel that this is *their* goal in the sense that they have accepted it. We have found that goals are most often accepted if the individual members can come together in a group, freely discuss their opinions concerning these goals, and take part in defining the steps by which these goals will be accomplished.

In the pages that follow, we have brought together some of the more useful material to help us understand the process of, and the problems involved in, obtaining supervisory participation in making changes. Our discussion is focussed on budgets simply because they are the topic at hand, *and not* because budgets are unique in the kinds of human problems that are related to them. Budgets, we all recognize, are but *one* of the many administrative processes which bring forth the kinds of human reactions described in this report.

Keeping in mind, therefore, that budgets are used primarily as a framework to present this new body of ideas, we shall suggest some concrete principles which may be helpful in bringing about participation in instituting a change.

Obtaining Acceptance of Budget Changes

1. Bring the supervisors together in small face-to-face groups.

2. Bear in mind that we are *not* just "selling them a new budget." We are also trying to "unsell" the old one . . . . the very budget we tried to sell last year. Each supervisor has built up a set of feelings, attitudes, and values concerning the existing budget. These have to be understood by the leader. They need to be brought out into the open and examined by the group members. An attempt to force the supervisors to create a new set of attitudes, feelings, and values might well place the supervisor in conflict. First of all, he won't like not having his old feelings respected. Second, a new set of attitudes might well be in conflict with the old. (An example of this occurs when top management completely changes the way it has been budgeting certain items.)

Therefore, any change that is introduced involves these steps:

a. Finding out the supervisor's present feelings, attitudes, and values concerning the present budget system.

b. Helping him, through his group, "unfreeze" these old feelings, attitudes, and values.

c. Helping him, through his group, discuss and accept, for the moment, the new feelings, attitudes, and values that will be attached to the new budget. This is done by helping the group as a *whole* accept these new attitudes.

d. Helping him, through his group, "freeze" the new set of attitudes, values, and feelings concerning the new budget.

e. Helping him make this supervisory group the kind of group in which a supervisor can feel that he is a member, and also feel, that he is an individual. When we join groups freely, we do so because they help us be what we are or want to be, and not ordinarily because we want to become hidden in something "greater" (i.e., the group).

The reader may question the emphasis on attitudes, feelings, and values about the budget. He may feel that there should be more initial emphasis on the acceptance of the figures *per se*.

Our emphasis is an outgrowth of the research. Time and time again, we found supervisors were not really resisting the new figures *per se*. (Assuming the figures were considered fair.) They were resisting because of some attitudes and/or feelings they had about the company, or their work group, or the finance office, or the budget supervisors or about the very way in which the figures were introduced.

It is true that they expressed their resistance by insisting the figures weren't fair, or that they couldn't understand them. But these reasons were often skin-surface, manifest reasons. They were *symptoms* of resistance, *not causes* of resistance.

In order that such a group can be created, the supervisors need to be able to drop their masks of caution and suspicion and learn to expect "honest and sincere" participation. All too often, industrial committees are groups whose members are always "being nice to each other," especially to the top brass. Each member hides his real feelings concerning others (i.e., he doesn't criticize his boss, nor will he criticize his fellow supervisors for fear that may look like he's "bucking"). Supervisors will accept real membership in a group (and therefore, the new values, goals, etc., of the group) when they are able to sense that the people accept them as they are.

3. It is best not to begin by introducing the change. This is too often what is done. Many of the controllers told us that they felt a good liaison man to institute the changes was one who could *sell* the changes. They described him as a man who could "speak the line-supervisor's language, and show him, tell him, what the new setup is."

We suggest, that before anyone attempts to sell something, he attempt to get the "buyer" to see the *need* for the product. And this is not done by *telling* the buyer how good the product is. It is probably more effectively done by helping the buyer to bring out the faults of the old. Once the supervisor has admitted the faults of the old, it will be easier for him to accept a system that attempts to do away with these faults.

4. "Patience is the god of progress." Introducing a new budget, as we have already suggested, is more than just introducing a new set of figures, a new accounting system. It also forces the supervisors to change their old and already accepted feelings, attitudes, and values, and their way of behaving. Introducing budgets, therefore, affects the very way people feel and behave.

After all, we as the "budget changers" undoubtedly took hours of work and much patience to get the budget into shape and to accept it ourselves. Why should we expect it to be different for the supervisors? This, incidentally, suggests that it might be a good idea *not* to have the new system all "packaged up" before it is shown to supervisors, as many finance people suggest. It might even be a good idea to let supervisors in on the original planning and headaches. Then, they develop with the budget. When it comes time to introduce it, it will not be something new and strange. It will already be partially theirs.

5. Finally, the leader might also try to handle the supervisors as individuals in a social group. We have noted above that supervisors belong to groups. These groups are important to them. These groups form the basis of their acceptance of, and behavior in certain specific ways. The person who wants to obtain effective participation from a supervisor, and attempts to obtain this participation solely by seeing the supervisor "individually," may find himself creating resistance, rather than reducing it. Certain things are best changed when the individuals are with their group. Acceptance of new budget systems seems to be one of these. Supervisors might tend to look with suspicion when they are called individually into the controller's office to discuss "their part" in the new plan.

Moreover, a supervisor directs only one part of an organization. His part usually cannot function effectively unless the other supervisors cooperate. Obviously, an organization is not made up of individual supervisors in isolation, but is composed of supervisors in certain human relationships with each other. These relationships must not be overlooked. They are important and should, therefore, be brought into the picture when any change is to be instituted.

Obtaining Acceptance at the Supervisors' Meeting

We have listed in the above sections a few broad suggestions which may help executives institute budget changes. Once the executive is face to face with the supervisors what additional steps should he take to make the changes acceptable? Here again, these suggestions can become useful guides only when they are tried and tested in individual situations. The business organization is, after all, our only laboratory.

These steps have proved helpful in some situations:

1. The executive first determines if the supervisors really see the need for the new system or for the changes in the old. He then determines how ready the supervisors are for the change.

If the supervisors do not see a need for the change, then the executive's job is to help the supervisors become willing to consider the change. As we have already pointed out this is not done through "selling" the new system. It is best done by permitting the supervisors to express themselves freely about their positive feelings for the old system and/or their negative feelings for the new system. Once these feelings are expressed and accepted, the men will feel less defensive since they spoke freely and they were not criticized.

Encouraging this free discussion helps the executive know the group resources available to help him make the change and the barriers the group will use to resist the change.

2. The executive encourages and supports the supervisors in building up a picture of what they can "get out of" the new plan. The advantages and limitations are listed and discussed. The executive tries to have the group list these advantages and disadvantages.

He, of course, may make contributions to both lists. He is careful, however, not to be the first contributor. If possible, he waits until the end and then adds those that have not been mentioned.

3. The next step seems to be to help the group make a step-by-step plan of the best way to introduce the new system. The executive helps them examine all the consequences of each step of the plan. Finally, he helps the group provide for replanning and constant assessment of the plan at each step.

This is also the time to emphasize "giving the new system a chance" to work before we criticize it.

4. The executive then helps the group members list the resources they feel they have or could obtain as individuals or as a group to make this change easier and more effective.

5. Finally, the executive creates a feeling on the part of all the group members that they are responsible for active participation.

These suggestions—cut to fit the individual situation—should help create *active acceptance* of budget changes through a process of *active participation*.

Training in Human Relations

The second area in which we should like to make some suggestions for action concerns training in human relations.

The interviews with the top controllers constantly emphasized the "figure conscious," narrow-minded rigidity of most finance people. For example:

> Most of them [*accountants*] are warped and they have narrow ideas. That, incidentally, is one of the failures of our educational system. We give the fellows all the textbook stuff but we never teach them how to sell accounting.

> Most of our accountants are narrow and short-sighted. They have a narrow breadth of view. They are what I call "shiny pants bookkeepers." They're technicians. They don't know how to handle people.

> I might add right here and now, that I think one of the worst human problems we have is the poor job of selling that is done with cost records and budgetary control. I think our accounting people are very, very poor in ability to get along with people and to sell them correctly. In fact, I'd go as far as to say the better the accountant, the poorer he is in human relations. I feel quite strongly about this.

Training in the Schools

The data indicate that more instruction in human relations needs to be given to students of cost accounting and budgeting at the college level. We are not prepared to say in what form this instruction can best be integrated into the curriculum, though it appears that such instruction could well be fitted into the traditional case approach of accounting instruction. The accounting and cost control cases usually present to the student some major technical problems for solution. At the end of each case the student is asked to answer certain questions. These questions could well include some concerning the human relations implications of the problem.

Training in Industry

Turning our attention to the training needed for the finance staff in industry, the writers doubt that the main training job is to train them to know the factory people's tasks. To do such a job thoroughly would require a lengthy and extremely expensive training program since the finance person would be required to learn the work of many people. Many plants have attempted to have the finance people visit the factory departments and learn some of the factory people's problems. This training has helped but it does not seem to have solved the problem.

The training should be focussed more on underlying problems rather than skin-surface ones. Some of the latest problems were suggested in the analysis. Recalling those for a moment, we might make the following specific suggestions:

1. The training should be focussed to help the finance staff perceive the human implications of the budget system.

2. The training should help show the finance staff the effects of pressure upon people. Thorough discussions seem necessary to understand the advantages and disadvantages of applying pressure on people.

3. Coupled with the discussions concerning pressure, the training should include discussions concerning the effects of success and failure. The accounting staff should be helped to perceive their difficult position, namely, that of placing others in "failure." They should also be taught the symptoms of people in failure. Finally, the course should include practical techniques which the finance staff can use to get along better with the factory people, knowing full well they (finance) may place these factory people in failure.

4. The human relations training should include thorough discussions of the human problems related to the department-centeredness of supervisors that are partially caused by budgets. The finance people should be helped to perceive this department-centeredness as a defense on the part of the factory supervisors rather than "narrow-mindedness," as some finance people have suggested.

5. Finally, there needs to be some instruction in the basic content of human relations as a field of study. This includes the concepts of informal and formal organizations, industrial organizations as social systems, status systems in industrial organizations, and such subjects as interviewing, counseling, and leadership.

Consideration of these subjects should help the financial staff become more aware of the human problems existing in organizations. Such an awareness is important since it is, as we have already suggested, the first step toward understanding the actions of ourselves and of others in the organization.

Suggestions for Further Research

What research remains to be done to provide more insight into the total problem area of human relations in budgets? Our experience in this exploratory study suggests questions listed below. They are merely an indication of some possible directions toward which new research may be aimed. The questions raised cannot be answered easily, but if future researchers have at their command the same degree of cooperation as that exhibited by members of Controllers Institute in sponsoring and participating in the present study, we are hopeful that answers can be found.

Future researchers should have as their goal (a) the discovery of additional aspects of the problem, and (b) the interrelationships of these aspects. In other words, more research is needed to identify all of the parts of the problem and how these parts are interrelated with each other.

Future research should also be directed at showing the interrelationships of this problem area with the total social system of the plant. Budget problems do not exist in isolation. "Budget problems," for all we know, may be caused by many factors other than financial ones. For example, in some plants, we have indications that "budget problems" are merely symptomatic expressions of deeper, underlying problems that permeate the entire plant social system. In such cases, the data suggest that budgets may well be the "scapegoat" or the "valve" through which a lot of pent-up feelings can be expressed.

More specifically, the following topics seem pertinent for further research:

What are the effects of success and failure upon factory supervisors as created by budgets in different plants?

How do the factory supervisors' attitudes affect the work done by the financial staff? How do their attitudes strengthen or weaken the administration of the budgets?

How much pressure can be applied without causing undue human tension and frustration? Exactly what does happen to a work group when they feel they are under pressure from the budget staff? If they unite against this pressure, how does this unification occur?

What are the best ways to reduce the forces of pressure and still obtain satisfactory production? How can the forces that prevent production from rising be weakened so that greater pressure is not needed to increase the production?

What happens to the supervisor if he cannot pass down the pressure he receives from above?

What are the best techniques by which one can eliminate some of the department-centeredness of the supervisors caused partially by budgets?

What value is there in training factory supervisors to understand accounting procedures? Similarly, what value is there in training the financial staff to be familiar, in a general manner, with the production processes?

Finally, what are the best methods by which genuine and whole-hearted participation can be obtained from the factory supervisors in the use of budgets?

OTHER FOUNDATION PUBLICATIONS

MANAGEMENT PLANNING FOR CORPORATE TAXES

This report is designed primarily as a "selling document,"—a thought starter for top financial management as to how to manage taxes. It is not a substitute for commercial services on taxation; it is not designed for the use of lawyers, accountants or tax experts. The report deals with corporate organization and executive attitudes and viewpoints.

(1951) $4.00

Controllers Institute Members $3.00

DEFENSE MOBILIZATION: What Management is Doing

Based on interviews with 35 companies who are doing something about meeting the impact of industrial mobilization, and on interviews with key personnel in Washington. The report contains an extensive Preparedness Check List for Management compiled by the Munitions Board.

(1951) $1.00

Controllers Institute Members $ .50

BUSINESS CONSULTANTS: Their Uses and Limitations

Based on experiences of 61 companies, this study answers these questions: What are the pertinent facts about consultants? Why do companies use consultants? How do companies choose consultants? How do companies get their money's worth?

(1951) $3.00

Controllers Institute Members $1.50

FACTS AND FIGURES FOR COLLECTIVE BARGAINING: The Controller's Role

A case history study based on the experience of over 40 companies. Tells what facts to give, what records to keep to tell management's side of the story in labor negotiations, arbitrations and fact-finding investigations.

(1950) $5.00

Controllers Institute Members $3.50

SETTING SALARIES IN THE CONTROLLER'S DEPARTMENT

A manual that is much more than a manual—Takes the guess work out of job pricing and giving raises. Contains detailed instructions on how to set salaries scientifically. Draws from the methods used by 22 companies and the salary scales used by 500 companies. Aims specifically at middle management jobs in the controller's department.

(1950) $10.00

Controllers Institute Members $7.50

BUSINESS FORECASTING

What can forecasting do for your business? Can accurate forecasting be done in your company? How can it be done? This report helps you to answer these questions by bringing you the detailed experiences of 38 companies which have found business forecasting an indispensable tool of management.

(1950)

(out of print)

MEETING THE CHALLENGE OF THE BUYER'S MARKET

This study describes actual cost reduction methods used by leading corporations in a wide cross section of industry. It is designed to help controllers and other executives do a better job in this direction. Case histories provide the bulk of this "brass tacks" information.

(1949) $5.00

Controllers Institute Members $2.50

EVALUATING MANAGERIAL AND SUPERVISORY JOBS IN THE CONTROLLER'S DEPARTMENT

This study makes it possible for the controller to apply scientific principles of job evaluation to managerial positions in his department. Based on intensive research into the methods of 12 leading corporations.

(1949)

(out of print)

CONTROLLERSHIP IN MODERN MANAGEMENT

A symposium written by twelve specialists. Traces the evolution and development of controllership in business and government. Tells how industry and educational institutions can recruit and prepare the controller of the future.

(1949) $6.65

Controllers Institute Members $5.00

DEPRECIATION POLICY WHEN PRICE LEVELS CHANGE

As a service to the business community, Controllership Foundation assembled a compendium of the principal authoritative opinions, case histories of company actions, and collections of information on this subject.

(1948) $2.00

Controllers Institute Members $1.00

WHAT PEOPLE WANT TO KNOW ABOUT YOUR COMPANY

A public opinion study to find out what "run of the mine" stockholders, women investors, large investors, financial analysts, employees and labor unions want to know about your company. The report discusses why the different publics are dissatisfied with financial reports and what to do about it.

(1948) $5.00

Controllers Institute Members—Free

DISTINGUISHING GOOD FROM NOT-SO-GOOD ACCOUNTING RESEARCH

Robert N. Anthony
Professor, Harvard University
Boston, Mass.

I owe you an explanation for the rather offbeat title of this talk. The original plan was that I would talk about Accounting Research. However, the more I thought about this vast subject, the less able I felt to summarize either the present state of research or of some facet of it. In searching for a way out, it occurred to me that as users of the results of accounting research, we all face the problem of sifting through the tremendous quantities of literature to find useful new ideas, and that it might be fruitful for us to think about efficient ways of going at this task.

If we are to get anywhere at all with this subject, we must adopt a somewhat broader definition of research than Carman Blough gave this morning. That definition is applicable to the physical or biological sciences where research consists either of experiments or of clinical observations that tend to prove or disprove a hypothesis. In a research hospital, a researcher thinks of a new type of operation that he hopes will cure children born with a certain type of abnormality. He experiments, first with animals, then with children, and he reports in the professional journals to his colleagues the results of these experiments. At the Children's Hospital in Boston, for example, the doctors have been experimenting with ways of saving babies born with an obstruction of the esophagus, a defect which had led to death within two weeks after birth in every case in recorded history. In the 1930's, they worked on 100 such cases, and in every one of them the baby died. But a complete description of their procedures, and their suggestions for the future, were nevertheless fully reported in the medical literature. Then, in 1939, they had their first success. After 44 operations, and 1,100 days of hospitalization, a little girl recovered (and incidentally is alive and healthy today), and this was reported. Currently, I am told the procedure has been improved to the point where it requires only one operation and three weeks in the hospital, and there is an 80 per cent chance of success.

There is nothing in business comparable with this type of research and reporting. Rarely is there any mention in our literature of procedures which were tried and did not work. And even reports on successes are not documented in a way that would satisfy a medical researcher. We need not explore the reasons for the difference here, other than to point out that the anatomy and physiology of a business are vastly more complicated than those of a human being. But if we are to have any basis for discussing research in business, or in accounting, clearly we must have a different definition than the scientific one. I see no point, for our present purpose, in trying to be more specific than the statement: Accounting research is what is described in a serious paper or book on accounting.

So, let us assume that we have before us a journal article on an accounting topic of interest. It is of interest either because as businessmen or future businessmen we hope it may provide a new idea for the successful operation of our business; or because as advisers to business, it may be something of interest to our clients; or because as teachers, it may represent something that should be incorporated in our instruction. How can we decide whether the idea in the article actually is worthwhile?

I shall discuss this question under three headings: the journal, the author, and the evidence.

The Journal

Some readers place a great deal of faith in certain magazines. Now although I am proud to be a member of its Editorial Board, I cringe at the statement: "It must be so because I read it in the *Harvard Business Review.*" We make no claim about the validity of our articles; indeed, we specifically disclaim any responsibility for the ideas in them. The current issue, for example, has an article on return on investment which in my personal opinion has completely fallacious conclusions. In the editor's opinion, however, the point of view of this article is one that businessmen should know about, and it is well argued. These are good enough reasons for running the article but the mere fact that it is run is not a good enough reason for believing it.

What, then, can the reader count on from the magazine itself? I think that the most that can be said is that if the magazine has a competent and a large enough editorial staff, you can have reasonable confidence in the factual accuracy of its contents: the numbers should add up, the equations should be in fact equal, the dates and other verifiable facts should be correct. But you cannot always expect even this. The *N.A.A. Bulletin*, for example, relies on manuscripts sent in by publications directors of its 150 chapters; each chapter must send in a certain number or it loses points in the annual chapter competition, and the harassed publications directors therefore try to pressure members to writing something—anything—to earn these points. From this flood of material, the editor in New York must pick 8 or 10 pieces every month to fill up the magazine. In such a rat race, it is scarcely surprising that there is a wide variation in the quality of articles, or that factual errors creep in.

All editors, being human beings, have biases, and sometimes a recognition of these can be useful in appraising the articles they run. This is a delicate point, and for safety's sake I shall illustrate it not with an accounting publication, but with the *Reader's Digest*. *Reader's Digest* articles tend to give the impression that there is nothing good about Russia, or China, or indeed most foreign countries, or most labor unions, or with (in quotation marks) the "government bureaucracy," and so on. It is not that their facts are incorrect; it is just that there is likely to be another side to the story that *Digest* articles omit.

The Author

If we see an article by someone we know and respect we naturally pay a great deal of attention to it. But suppose, as is usually the case, that the author is unknown to me. I then think it is quite important to find out about both (a) his background, and (b) his bias, before considering what he has written. I emphasize *both* background and bias. The partner of a public accounting firm, I assume, has a very good background in the accounting area, but if he writes an article describing a new technique his firm has developed and would like to sell to clients,I rather suspect that he is emphasizing the virtues and minimizing the weaknesses of this technique, and I read the article accordingly. Similarly, a press release describing the wonders of the new Model 999 computer is to be read somewhat differently from a reasoned analysis of the performance of such a computer by a graduate student, even through the graduate student has much less background on the subject.

An excellent example of how differences in point of view affect articles appeared in recent issues of the *Harvard Business Review*. In the March 1959 issue, we ran an article by Donald Gant arguing that long-term noncancelable leases are equivalent to debt, and that companies are greatly overrating their attractiveness as a means of financing. In the May 1959 issue, we had a strong rejoinder by Alvin Zises. In order to understand these articles, I think it is absolutely essential that the reader recognize that Donald Gant works for Goldman Sachs & Co., an investment banking firm, whose business of underwriting bond issues has not been helped by the growth of leasing, and that Alvin Zises is President of the Bankers Leasing Corporation. In saying this, I am not disparaging either the articles or their authors. As a matter of fact, I think Gant's article was the best one we ran in 1959. What I mean is that if one reads these pieces without keeping in mind the background and bias of their respective authors, he is not in a good position to make an intelligent evaluation of their contents.

Theoretically, professors should have the least bias of any group. They have nothing to sell, no axe to grind. Unfortunately, this theory does not always work out in practice, but even if it did, professors also tend to have inadequate backgrounds for dealing with the realities of business.

In January, 1953 for example, we ran an article by Professor Chris Argyris,[1] a social scientist, which was very critical of current budgeting practices. If you go back to the article, you will find that it was based on a study of three manufacturing plants. Careful reading of the article will show that all three of these plants used the old-fashioned *imposed* type of budget, one dictated by top management without the full participation of the operating personnel. It is therefore no surprise that the budget did not produce good results in these three companies. But Argyris, although undoubtedly unbiased, did not at that time know enough about business to realize that his selection of these three particular plants practically guaranteed that he would get the results he did get.

If professors of accounting could be as close to business as medical researchers are to their hospital patients, their reports would be ideal, but the facts of life are such that this is usually not the case.

The Evidence

We can classify accounting articles into four categories: (a) those not based on any evidence; (b) those based on the evidence of one company's experience; (c) those based on surveys; and (d) those based on experiments. I am intentionally omitting articles that use as evidence quotations drawn from the literature since we are interested in articles that describe new ideas, rather than a compilation of other people's ideas.

This paper is, frankly, an example of the first category. It contains no evidence to support its points, and you must therefore judge it in terms of whether the ideas seem plausible, whether the arguments are logical, and whether they jibe with your own experience. So it is with all similar articles, and these comprise a large fraction of those in the literature. I shall not dwell further on this category in general, but I do want to mention a special subcategory, operations research.

[1] Chris Argyris, "Human Problems with Budgets," *Harvard Business Review*, Jan.-Feb. 1953, pp. 97–110.

An operations researcher tries to construct a mathematical model of a business or some part of a business. By definition, this model cannot be an exact duplicate of the situation it purports to describe. The researcher must necessarily make simplifying assumptions in order to make the mathematics manageable, and having done so, he can make his computations and describe the results in an article in a publication like *Management Science* or *Operations Research*. These mathematical calculations are by no means the same thing as evidence. The mathematics should show precisely what will happen in the *assumed* situation, but what we are interested in is not the assumed situation, but the real life situation that is being modeled. The only way I know of to find out whether the mathematics is applicable to real life is to try out the results in a real situation and see what happens.

Thus, I am not very much impressed by a mathematical demonstration that has not been tried out in real life. Indeed, the first thing I do in looking at an OR article is to see if there has been an actual trial of the results. I may in fact miss some revolutionary new idea this way, but I save a lot of mental torture in wading through the formulas.

We professors run into this problem all the time with student reports. Just recently a colleague was telling me about a very elaborate scheme a student had worked out for determining how much a company should spend on advertising. The student took his proposal to the management of the company he was working with, and they studied it with some care and finally said: "This may or may not be quite valuable. Before we can judge it we need to have you tell us how we can get the numbers to fit into the equations you have built up." "Oh," said the student, "my job was to develop the equations; it's your job to find the proper numbers to fit into them." And since these numbers were nowhere in existence, that was the end of that.

This problem is by no means confined to students. My favorite example is a very learned article from the magazine *Operations Research* which applied probability theory, queuing theory, and Monte Carlo techniques to the problem of handling freight cars in railroad classification yards.[2] The researchers found that in the current practice, two operations were performed one after the other. First, the incoming cars were inspected for mechanical defects, and, next, they were classified into trains by shunting or humping them to the proper track. The conclusion of the mathematical analysis was that the railroad could save time and money ($100,000 a year) by carrying out the inspection at the same time that

[2] Roger R. Crane, Frank B. Brown, and Robert O. Blanchard, "An Analysis of a Railroad Classification Yard," *Operations Research*, Vol. 3, August 1955, p. 262.

the car was being humped. The researchers, however, did not make the slightest effort to find out whether the inspectors were in fact willing and able to inspect the cars while they were in motion, nor what new costs would be involved in transporting the inspectors back and forth. Without evidence on these points, the whole mathematical analysis is worthless.

Company Experience

The second category of evidence is that based on company practice. Now, I suppose that a true scientist would ordinarily not pay much attention to an idea supported by only one experiment. In business, however, we often do pay attention to results of this kind, and I think with good reason. If the new technique works, and *if* it works for the reasons we have postulated, this is a powerful argument in its favor. The catch is in the second "if." Why does the new idea work? Is it because it was an inherently sound idea, or was it for some other reason that we do not know about? The classic example of experimenters being misled by the evidence is the so-called bank-wiring studies at Western Electric many years ago. You will recall that the experiment increased the lighting in a room where women were wiring banks of telephone switchboards, and that with each increase in lighting there was a corresponding increase in productivity. The natural conclusion was that in order to get good productivity, you had to have good lighting. However, as a final experiment, they decreased the light levels to what they were when the experiments began, and to their surprise they found that productivity, instead of dropping, actually increased again. Eventually they concluded that it was not the lighting that caused the increase in productivity, but rather a reason that they had not even been studying, namely, the workers were impressed by the fact that the experimenters showed an interest in improving their performance.

This problem arises whenever an accounting technique influences or is influenced by the reactions of human beings. Thus, I am cautious about automatically attributing improvements in cost control, or whatever, to the particular technique being described in the article, and I would very much appreciate a description of the steps taken by the author to investigate whether the reported advantages are actually the results of the new technique, or whether they come from some other causal force. This is the basic weakness with nearly all articles on the topic of direct costing, for example.

The question of bias also comes up with this one-company evidence, of course. The person who thinks up a new idea and tries it out in practice is quite naturally fond of his brainchild. It is unreasonable to expect him to be completely objective about it, to seek out and confess publicly the weaknesses or qualifications that may lessen the apparent advantages. For this reason, the report of an outsider carries much more weight with me than the report of an actual participant in the experiment.

Often, it is not easy to determine whether or not the article does report actual practice. An article from the March 1960 *N.A.A. Bulletin* is a case in point.[3] The author is a systems analyst in a company, and some of his illustrative forms look like regular company forms, but nowhere does he say that his company is using the technique described. And this is a crucial matter, because he is describing a complicated technique for controlling research and development. A key question about such techniques always is the matter of whether the engineers have the ability and the willingness to make the detailed forecasts that are required. In the absence of definite assurance that these techniques have been tried and found practical, I must classify them as just another system man's pipe dream, and an engineer's nightmare.

Evidence from Surveys

Next, we come to evidence based on surveys. This is a subject on which many books have been written, and instead of attempting an orderly treatment of it, I intend to give only three practical criteria that seem to me particularly useful in judging whether to attach any meaning to the results of a survey.

First, I want some evidence that the investigator worked hard on the survey. A good survey is expensive. The questions must be written, discussed, tested, and rewritten. The best possible list of people or companies must be thought about and located. Followups and tests of nonrespondents must be planned and faithfully carried out. Analyzing the responses is much more than a mechanical job of tabulation. When an article describes a survey and the only statement about the survey process is "executives of fifteen corporations with a reputation for experience with profit planning were interviewed," with not one word about the selection of these companies, the length of the interview, the questions asked, or the particular persons seen, I am pretty hesitant to accept the reported results as having any meaning.

Second, I want to see the actual questions so I can make my own interpretation of what the answers mean. I have read three recent surveys on the extent to which companies use return on investment. One reports

[3] Cecil R. Hollis, "Programming for Control of Contract Performance," *N.A.A. Bulletin*, Section 1, March 1960, p. 19.

60 per cent[4] of respondents use the technique, the second reports 78 per cent[5] and the third reports 100 per cent.[6] One asked the vague question: "Does your company use the return on investment concept as a management tool?" In another, the exact question asked is not given in the report. The great difference between these results can easily be accounted for by the different ways in which the question was asked.

Incidentally, it is surprising how many investigators fail to distinguish between what the respondents say they do, and what they actually do, yet the existence of this difference is a well-known fact of life. In a recent survey on long-term leasing, for example, we asked investment analysts: "What procedure do you normally use to evaluate these lease obligations?" Seventy-seven per cent of our 256 respondents stated that they normally included lease payments as a fixed charge in computing coverage, or that they capitalized lease payments in computing balance sheet ratios, or both.[7] We thereupon sent 163 of these people a set of four little problems and asked them to make the calculations they normally make. From the responses to this second-stage survey, we estimate that considerably less than half of these people actually do use the techniques they said they used. The explanation is simple: on the first survey, many people checked the technique they thought they *ought* to use.

Third, for obvious reasons, I want to know the size and composition of the sample and of the respondents.

Given the above three pieces of information: good data about the survey process, the exact questions asked, and the survey size and composition, I usually can make up my mind about whether a survey has anything useful for me. Note that I have not mentioned tests of randomness of the sample, the size of the standard deviations, or other such matters which are discussed in courses in statistical sampling. These techniques are of crucial importance in public opinion polls, and I would pay no attention to a public opinion poll that did not handle them correctly. But in surveys of business practice, they are nowhere near as important. Other things being equal, a probability sample is a good thing, but the matters outside the straight statistics are usually much more important than statistical elegance. In fact, I know of one large government survey, involving hundreds of thou-

[4] Professor Dennis Gordon, University of Akron, Responses from 200 companies.

[5] Eugene Ladin, "Return on Investment Concept Applied to Air Force Central Procurement," Student Research Program of School of Business, Air University, August 1959. Responses from 76 companies.

[6] "Return on Capital as a Guide to Managerial Decisions," NAA Research Report 35, 1959, p. 6. Responses from 44 companies.

[7] Richard F. Vancil and Robert N. Anthony, "The Financial Community Looks at Leasing," *Harvard Business Review*, Nov.-Dec. 1959, pp. 113-130.

sands of dollars of money and thousands of respondents, that was severely crippled by the statistician's insistence on a universe defined in such a way that he could draw a random sample from it, rather than in a way that made sense in terms of the phenomena being studied.

Of course, the percentage of respondents to a survey who report the adoption of a new technique is not too important anyway. We are interested in new ideas, and if we wait until a *majority* of companies have acted, we shall be quite a way behind the leaders. The best guide, I think, is "Be not the first by whom the new is tried, nor yet the last to cast the old aside."

Evidence Based on Experiment

If business is to become a science, and if business research or accounting research is to have a meaning comparable to what it has in the physical and biological sciences, then my final category of evidence (evidence based on experiment) must eventually become the most important of all. Unfortunately, there is so far only a tiny amount of such research; and of the amount that is done, only a fraction is done by people who understand accounting or business well enough so that we can profit by the results.

I shall mention two examples. One is a study made by Jack Grayson at Harvard.[8] This is the very first set of actual experiments bearing on the question of whether businessmen can in fact estimate a reasonable utility function, something which they must be able to do if the new statistical decision rules involving utility are to have any practical application. The second is the study by Andrew Stedry of Carnegie Tech.[9] Here is a pioneering attempt to test by actual experiments the validity of some of the long-standing folklore people have had about budgeting. For example, is there actually some advantage in having a tight budget over a loose budget? Although I cannot entirely agree with the validity of the experimental evidence or of the mathematics given in other parts of Stedry's study, these possible weaknesses are nowhere near as important as the fact that the attempt was made. These are examples of the type of research we need much more of.

Conclusion

In my comments and examples above, you will note that I have confined myself to management accounting, and have said nothing about re-

[8] Charles Jackson Grayson, Jr., *Decisions Under Uncertainty: Drilling by Independent Oil and Gas Operators.* (Harvard University Graduate School of Business Administration. George F. Baker Foundation), September 1958.

[9] Andrew C. Stedry, *Budget and Control and Cost Behavior*, May 1959.

search in financial accounting theory. This was intentional, since the two problems are quite different. In fact, I doubt that much useful research in financial accounting is possible until the profession has made up its collective mind as to what the basic ground rules—the postulates—of accounting are to be.

Let me recapitulate: Your attention is attracted to a new idea in an article, and you are trying to make up your mind as to whether the idea has merit. I have suggested that you cannot get much help from the prestige or reputation of the magazine itself, but must rely principally on your appraisal of the author and of his evidence. I have suggested that in all cases where the author is unknown to you, evaluation of his bias and background is essential. With respect to the evidence, I have urged a sharp distinction between a theoretical description of "what might be" versus a report of what actually happened, either in a single company or in a group of companies.

You may note an underlying tone of dissatisfaction with the state of accounting research. I *am* dissatisfied. Powerful forces are at work to push a tremendous volume of worthless material out upon us: the pressure on professors to "publish or perish," the childish point system of the National Association of Accountants, the belief on the part of firms that publications is an effective form of advertising, the absence of any professional standards of what constitutes acceptable research in accounting, the lack of a system of professional review of manuscripts, the unwillingness of the business community to support the expensive and time-consuming process that is essential to sound research, and so on. The recent N.A.A. statement of *Objectives and Methods of Research in Management Accounting* adds to this feeling of dissatisfaction. We must have higher sights and higher standards than those outlined in that document if we are to make real progress.

The Grayson and Stedry projects mentioned above are two gleams on the horizon, signs of what I hope will be a much stronger tendency in the future. But the question of how to hasten that happy day would start me off again, and it is time to stop talking.

TENTATIVE STATEMENT OF COST CONCEPTS UNDERLYING REPORTS FOR MANAGEMENT PURPOSES

COMMITTEE ON COST CONCEPTS AND STANDARDS

AMERICAN ACCOUNTING ASSOCIATION

TENTATIVE STATEMENT OF COST CONCEPTS UNDERLYING REPORTS FOR MANAGEMENT PURPOSES

COMMITTEE ON COST CONCEPTS AND STANDARDS

EXPLANATORY NOTE: The concepts set forth in this statement are not standards for the cost accounting procedures of recording historical cost. They represent concepts of the costs most useful to management for planning and control decisions. It is to be expected that in practical application, various techniques, procedures, and rules will be developed, of which historical cost recording is but one, to provide data representative of the costs suggested by these concepts. Often the representations of the basic costs will be rough approximations of varying degrees of reliability. The basic concepts of cost described in this statement serve two functions: First, they indicate desired measures of cost and thus serve as a basis for judging the reliability of any cost data provided to management for planning and control decisions. Second, they serve as an inducement to the development of improved techniques and procedures for supplying appropriate cost information to management.

The development of techniques and procedures to provide the most reliable approximations of the basic costs is beyond the scope of this statement. Such procedures and techniques may be expected to differ from enterprise to enterprise but the basic concepts of cost set forth here are the underlying concepts toward the realization of which the specific techniques and procedures strive. The basic concepts are believed to have rather general application.

PREFATORY NOTE

In June, 1936, the executive committee of the American Accounting Association issued a tentative statement of accounting principles underlying corporate financial statements. That statement and subsequent revisions suggested concepts and standards underlying the preparation of accounting reports on financial position and income. While reports of income and financial position are used by managements in reaching certain broad decisions, a far greater proportion of managerial decisions and actions are based upon other reports. This suggests the need for a statement of the concepts underlying these other reports.

For several years, work has been proceeding toward the development of a statement of cost concepts useful in the preparation of reports for management. Progress in this area has now reached a point where it seems desirable to issue a tentative statement of such cost concepts. This statement seems advisable to advance the following objectives:

(1) To stimulate further study and discussion of the accounting information needed by management.
(2) To suggest cost data which are pertinent to various types of management problems.
(3) To call attention to the broad and indefinite nature of cost as a general term and to reveal how appropriate costs depend upon the purpose for which they are to be used.
(4) To describe a portion of the field of accounting within a framework sufficiently broad to provide an insight into the problem of providing accounting information for management purposes.

The concepts set forth here represent a broad approach to the problem of business cost. As such they include concepts generally not appropriate for the determination of income and include costs which may not be a part of the basic accounting records. Essentially they suggest the most appropriate cost data for management uses. In this report attention is directed toward the development of underlying concepts. These concepts, in turn, may require further development of procedures and working approximations to effect their application in any given business situations.

THE NATURE OF BUSINESS COST

For business purposes, cost is a general term for a measured amount of value purposefully released or to be released in the acquisition or creation of economic resources, either tangible or intangible. Normally it is measured in terms of a monetary sacrifice involved. There is, however, nothing to prevent its measurement in other terms nor to prevent the adjustment of monetary sacrifices to common units of purchasing power. Conceptually, cost excludes distribution of capital and income as well as certain unexpected value releases.

Basic Framework

An understanding of the nature of cost requires comprehension of (a) the purposeful aspect of the term "cost," (b) the relationship of business risk to cost, and (c) methods of measuring value releases.

(a) To qualify as cost, the value release must be for the purpose of furthering a managerial objective. There are two aspects to this concept. First, only the value releases necessary for the acquisition or creation of economic resources to carry out a managerial objective are costs. Second, the amount released will depend upon the use to be made by management of the computed costs. Thus the cost of acquiring or creating economic resources for a managerial objective should include only those value releases necessary to carry out the specific objective. But, because the purpose in measuring the value releases may be to aid management in varying levels of planning and control decisions, the amount of value release will depend upon the use to be made of the computed costs. In somewhat comprehensive terms, the purposeful aspect of cost means that because managerial objectives vary both in scope of activity (ranging from overall activities to a multitude of minor activities) and in the nature of the management function being performed (ranging from planning to control), the value releases to be included in any cost report will vary with the situation of the firm as well as with the specific objective of management. In a broad sense, this recognizes that the cost of anything will depend upon the purpose for determining cost.

(b) Business operations necessarily involve risk. In some instances these risks are transferred to an insuror. In others, though not transferred, they are measured and allowed for as an element of cost. In still others, they cannot be foreseen or, if foreseen, are so uncertain that estimation is impractical. Value releases occasioned by the transfer of risk to an insuror, or by uninsured risk which lend themselves to measurement, are costs. Value releases occasioned by unforeseen, or highly uncertain, risks are not costs but should be considered in evaluating the risk of the operation. If incurred they are, of course, considered as losses in determining income.

(c) Normally, value releases due to operations are measured in monetary terms. The measurement of the monetary sacrifice involved in the acquisition or creation of economic resources is simplest when the value release is an outflow of cash. Adjustment for the timing of cash outflow is sometimes necessary and can be accomplished by discounting or advancing outflows at an appropriate rate of interest. Similarly, adjustment for changes in the purchasing power of money can be made by the use of appropriate price indexes. The needs of management for a report on monetary sacrifice, however, often require the measurement of noncash outflows. Most often such outflows result from the release of economic resources now on hand. It is in the measurement of these latter outflows that special difficulties arise.

Cost Classifications

Cost is classified normally in terms of a managerial objective. Its presentation normally requires sub-classification. Such sub-classification may be according to functional lines, areas of responsibility, the nature of the cost elements, or some other useful breakdown. The appropriate sub-classification depends upon the uses to be made of the cost report.

Uses of Business Cost Reports

Within the foregoing framework of the nature of cost, various concepts may be developed that are appropriate in the preparation of cost reports useful for business decisions.

Managerial functions may be grouped into the areas of (1) planning and (2) control. Cost concepts appropriate for each of these two areas are developed in this statement. In general, the cost concepts useful for planning are those relevant to a managerial decision on future action; whereas the cost concepts useful for control are those which aid in carrying out adopted plans. In addition, because the costs in accounting records are used by management as a basis for planning and control, it is advisable to set forth certain concepts which underlie these accounting costs. Accordingly, this statement deals with cost concepts appropriate for planning and for control, and with historical cost reports to management. The concepts set forth are somewhat ideal. Approximations of these basic concepts often must be used in business situations.

COSTS FOR PLANNING

Depending upon the purpose for which it is undertaken, all business planning may be classified as (1) project planning or (2) period planning. Project planning is the process whereby management, confronted by a specific problem, evaluates each alternative in order to arrive at a decision as to the course of future action.[1] Period planning is the process whereby management systematically develops an acceptable set of plans for the total future activities of the enterprise, or some functional subdivision thereof, for a specified period of time.

The two types of planning can and often do occur simultaneously. While some of the more important problems requiring project planning are apt to occur sporadically and involve alternatives of long and varying time periods, others follow the fixed time pattern of period planning. The second situation exists because management is able to control the length of time for which alternative commitments may be made, and chooses to employ the period planning cycle as that length of time. For this reason many activities entailed in the process of period planning are actually project planning. Wherever a selection between alternatives is necessary, project planning is involved.

COSTS FOR PROJECT PLANNING

Costs for project planning are estimates of future value releases anticipated as a result of adopting any one of the alternative courses of future action considered by

[1] In a broad sense project planning may be defined as the process of reaching a decision on future action. It may range from the least important decision of the least important worker to the broadest of decisions by the board of directors. As a process it may be described as (a) recognizing several possible courses of future action, (b) evaluating each alternative (in both monetary and non-monetary terms), and (c) expressing a decision to adopt one of the alternatives as the course of future action. Planning costs are concerned primarily with the evaluation process.

the company. Such costs are future costs which may be expressed as differential costs because evaluation is a comparative process requiring the determination of how total costs (and revenues) are likely to vary under different sets of future conditions.[2]

In estimating future differential costs of each of a given set of alternatives, it is necessary to recognize one alternative as the standard. Often this standard is the alternative which envisages mere continuation of the current plan. All services[3] required by each of the other alternatives which differ as to type, quantity, or time of release from those required by the standard must be determined and their future costs estimated.

In order to measure the future costs of these differential services, a distinction should be made between differential services on hand, or for which the company is irrevocably committed, at the beginning of the planning period, and those to be acquired within that period; between those expected to be entirely consumed within that period and those of which a residual is expected to remain at the end of the period; and between those which management considers replacing and those which it does not.

Furthermore, when the project planning period is long, it is necessary to adjust all differential costs in order to take account of significant time and risk variations. The most satisfactory method for doing this is by means of the discounting procedure.

[2] Any alternative may be analyzed by determining the total expected value release occasioned by all future activities of which it is but a part and comparing this cost with the total costs of other alternatives, determined in the same manner. Since many costs are common to every alternative, the comparison actually rests on the differences in total costs of the alternatives. In this "Tentative Statement of Cost Concepts" the more direct procedure is stressed. Only differential costs of the alternatives are to be measured and compared. The difference between the two methods is procedural, but care must be taken in the direct approach to ensure that important differences are not overlooked. There is less chance of making this kind of an error if the total cost procedure is used.

[3] The term "services" is sometimes used in a more narrow sense to refer to personal services but there seems no sound reason to restrict the term when it is evident that the purchase of either labor or physical assets is for the purpose of acquiring the services in these resources.

Differential Services to be Acquired and Fully Consumed

The basis for estimating future costs of differential services to be acquired and fully consumed within the planning period is the expected future outlay of cash, or its equivalent, required for their acquisition.

(1) When the cash outlay is expected to coincide with service acquisition and both will take place over a period of time, the proper measure of cost is the sum of the discounted amounts of (a) the initial outlay, (b) the complementary outlays required for realization of the initial outlay, and (c) any further outlay required to dispose of the acquisition.

(2) Often the outlay will be in the form of a promise to pay cash, or its equivalent, at a time subsequent to the service acquisition date. In this situation the value release as of the date of expected service acquisition should be measured by discounting the expected cash outlay to the date of service acquisition. A rate of interest equivalent to that required for borrowing money may be used for the discounting process. The resulting amount should be treated as in (1) above.

(3) At times the outlay will be in the form of services other than cash, or promises to pay cash. If replacement of such services is considered, the cash equivalent is measured by their estimated replacement cost, at the time of expected replacement discounted to the date of acquisitions. If replacement is not considered, cash equivalent is measured by the estimated net proceeds foregone (i.e., net selling price adjusted for estimated selling

costs) because of the exchange.[4] The resulting amount should be treated as in (1) above.

Differential Services to be Acquired and Partially Consumed

The basis for estimating future costs of differential services to be acquired and partially consumed during the project planning period is the future outlay of cash, or its equivalent, required for their acquisition, less the estimated cash equivalent valuation of services remaining at the end of the period.

(1) The measure of the cash, or its equivalent, for the acquisition of these services is the same as that used in measuring differential services acquired and fully consumed.
(2) If replacement of the remaining services is considered by management, their valuation can be measured by estimated replacement cost, at the time of expected replacement, discounted to the end of the period.
(3) If replacement of these residual services is not a present consideration, their valuation may be measured by estimated net proceeds as of the end of the period.

Differential Services on Hand and Fully Consumed

The basis for estimating future costs of differential services on hand, or for which the company is irrevocably commited, at the beginning of the period which are expected to be fully consumed within that period is their cash equivalent valuation at the time of utilization.

(1) If replacement of such services is considered by management, their valuation is estimated replacement cost at the time of utilization.
(2) If replacement of such services is not a consideration of management, their valuation is estimated net proceeds foregone at the time of utilization.

Differential Services on Hand and Partially Consumed

The basis for estimating future costs of differential services on hand, or for which the firm is irrevocably committed, at the beginning of the period which are expected to be partially consumed within that period is their cash equivalent valuation at the time of utilization.

(1) If replacement of such services is considered, their valuation is estimated replacement cost, at the date of expected replacement, discounted to the time of utilization.

Time, Risk and Uncertainty Adjustments

The future differential costs associated with each alternative must be adjusted for time, risk of loss, and uncertainty of risk before evaluation is possible. Discounting each anticipated future cost to some common point in time is usually the most satisfactory method of adjustment for time and risk factors. The rate(s) of discount used for these purposes should reflect management's appraisal of the risk entailed by each prospective undertaking.

If the time periods of two or more of the alternatives are significantly different, these differences must be taken into account in any calculation. One method of doing so is to compare the two alternatives on the basis of the rates of return implied by their respective investments and future net proceeds.

[4] The concept employed here is frequently called value in best alternative use. Where replacement is considered, the value in best alternative use is presumed to be a substitute for the cost of replacement. If the time period between the date of exchange and the date of expected replacement is long and storage costs are important, replacement cost at the time of expected replacement should be adjusted by the estimated differential storage costs saved through the proposed exchange.

If replacement is not considered, net proceeds is the higher of the remaining alternatives of: (1) sale as is; or (2) use in some other production or distribution activity. In the latter case, the value cannot exceed replacement cost.

Throughout this entire section, it is presumed that management's consideration of replacement reflects the fact that it is the best alternative. That is, it considers replacement only where the discounted replacement cost is in excess of net proceeds. If this assumption were dropped, the proper measure of cost would be discounted replacement cost or net proceeds whichever is the higher.

Another method is to select a common time period, preferably the shortest period, to which the firm would be committed by the adoption of any one of the alternatives. Each of the longer alternatives can then be fitted to the shortest period by estimating the cash equivalent valuation of the residual services as of the end of the common time period.

The degree of uncertainty attending each of the estimates of future differential cost for each of the various alternatives may be taken into account by employing different rates of discount, or setting forth a range for each set of estimates. Full disclosure of the bases for the estimates should be made to assist management in its evaluation.

Pricing

A special area of planning which warrants separate attention is pricing. Cost is one element in the determination of price, but it must be considered in concert with numerous other factors embodied in the total concept of demand.

In non-repetitive sales, the future differential cost of making and selling the product, measured from the costs of not making and selling the product, ordinarily establishes a lower limit for price. This limit may be ignored by management for short periods because of certain non-monetary factors, but the monetary sacrifice entailed in so doing is measured by the difference between price and future differential cost. It is management's responsibility to determine subjectively whether or not this sacrifice is warranted by non-monetary considerations.

In repetitive selling, many non-monetary factors such as competitive reactions, legal requirements, or ultimate needs for replacement, usually dictate a higher minimum than that embodied in any short period planning cost. Conceptually, the planning costs for pricing goods which are sold repetitively should take into account the discounted total future gains and losses occasioned by the adoption of any one price or price structure rather than another. Since most of these future gains and losses defy satisfactory expression in monetary terms, the selection of the margin of price over future differential costs is a direct responsibility of management.

COSTS FOR PERIOD PLANNING

The principal objective of period planning is the development of various sets of plans and their conversion into a single overall plan in order to direct and coordinate each of the separate activities and to assure that their summation is an acceptable whole. The period adopted usually is one year. The adopted plan is the basis for communication and includes cost data useful for control of subsequent operations.

Period planning usually results in an overall budget. Such planning ordinarily is carried on within the framework of anticipated costs and revenues for income determination purposes or other rather complete accumulations of costs rather than differential cost constructions. In this respect period planning represents a potential area of conflict between planning and income determination costs. For those activities whose future service requirements within the budget period will be consumed during the same period, the period planning employs essentially the same cost concepts as project planning. One difference is that for convenience project plans are often measured in terms of differential costs whereas period plans are stated in terms of rather complete accumulations of cost. In those activities for which services are on hand at the beginning or end of the planning period, the results of the two also may differ because period planning uses the booked cost valuations for income determination as opposed to the cost concepts appropriate for project planning purposes.

In many instances project planning is carried out as a part of period planning. In other instances, it is not feasible to subject all areas of the business at short intervals to a review and replanning of past adopted plans or to undergo project planning for all items. These latter items then enter into the planning process directly via period planning.

Normally, the process of period planning involves a build-up of estimated future costs by areas of responsibility and functions which must be performed if major policies and previously adopted plans are to be followed. Typically, the estimating procedure utilizes historical costs. The concept of variable cost is a useful device for such planning purposes, but it can be easily misinterpreted. Because it normally reflects the relationship of only one variable (volume) to the behavior of total costs, this concept is often inadequate, since expected changes in factors other than volume (e.g., price, efficiency, or management attitude) will have a significant effect upon future outlays. Variable cost may be used as a first approximation of future cost. Adjustments can be made to take account of expected changes in the other variable before final estimates are determined.

Period planning provides for an overall evaluation by top level management of a master plan prepared in accordance with major policies and restrictions previously imposed by it. It is constructed as a reviewing device rather than as a means of providing the basis for the preparation of another master plan or revision of the plan under consideration. Changes in planned combinations of activities, induced by apparently unsatisfactory total results presented in period planning, should be re-examined in the light of the proper concepts of project planning cost before they are effected.

The communication of adopted period plans normally envisions their construction in such a manner as to co-ordinate and control the activities of the firm. This involves the assignment of these period plans to areas of responsibility.

COSTS FOR CONTROL

Cost data are useful in the control of current operations. The selection of cost concepts for such purposes is a matter of personal discretion depending upon the cost construction which in the given situation is believed to be best able to accomplish the objectives. Therefore, such costs may be historical costs, standard costs, planning costs, or even constructions which merely simulate costs. They are useful for three main purposes:

(1) Costs are useful, along with other devices, as a means of communicating information about approved plans.
(2) Costs may be constructed and used in a way that will motivate individuals within the organization to take action most likely to further the interests of the firm.
(3) Costs are useful as a means of reporting actual performance and the differences between actual performance and the performance that should have been attained under the circumstances. These reports may provide a useful tool for improving performance in future periods.

Costs as a Communication Device

Cost data help to convey information about the objectives that management wishes to achieve, the methods to be used to achieve these objectives, and the limitations to which the organization is expected to adhere. These objectives, methods, and limitations are the result of decisions reached in the planning process. Cost data therefore are devices by means of which management can direct individuals within the organization to carry out plans. In this use, costs may be classified in terms of activity, personal responsibility, or types of services to be used in carrying out the adopted plans. While the budget is one form of communicating information of this type, it is, of course, not the sole means and rarely is it as important as other communication devices, particularly oral instructions.

The measurable concepts of cost appropriate for the communication function require a mutual understanding by management and individuals of the bases upon which the costs are calculated.

Costs as a Device for Motivation

Cost data, if properly constructed and if accompanied by proper management action and attitude, can be an important factor in motivating the organization, for they may serve as an incentive for accomplishing the planned objectives. Some concepts useful in developing cost data that help to motivate individuals within the organization may be suggested.

1. A basic concept of motivation is that it is best accomplished when costs are related to personal responsibility, but this does not mean that individuals should be charged only with costs for which they are completely responsible. There are few, if any, elements of cost that are the sole responsibility of one person. Some guides in deciding the appropriate costs to be charged to a person (responsibility center) are as follows:

(a) If the person has authority over both the acquisition and the use of the services, he should be charged with the cost of such services.
(b) If the person can significantly influence the amount of cost through his own action, he may be charged with such costs.
(c) Even if the person cannot significantly influence the amount of cost through his own direct action, he may be charged with those elements with which the management desires him to be concerned so that he will help to influence those who are responsible.

2. A method of motivation that may be useful is the designation of a cost limit to serve as a restriction on service acquisition or utilization for a specified activity. This approach is especially useful in areas where costs cannot be related to specific performance, such as research personnel, and other staff functions.

(a) The limitation may represent an inviolate ceiling or merely a statement of expectations around which a certain amount of latitude is permitted.
(b) The limitation may be expressed as a single amount or it may be broken down into detailed service categories depending upon the type of control that management wishes to exercise.

3. The basis of measurement used in providing cost data for control is often a matter of management discretion and an important consideration in motivation. Different bases may significantly affect the way in which different individuals are motivated. For this reason, the bases of measurement selected should be consistent with the type of motivation desired. For example, different types of motivation may result when maintenance costs are charged to a responsibility center on the bases of: (1) a rate per maintenance labor hour, (2) a rate per job, or (3) a single amount per month.

4. Reporting with respect to costs for which any person is held responsible should be consistent both as to basis for measuring any given cost factor and the types of cost factors included in such reports. This implies that if a budget includes labor costs measured on a standard basis, performance costs being compared with the budget should be measured according to the same standard. Likewise a person should not be held responsible for a cost factor in one report, and be freed from responsibility for the same factor in another report.

Costs as an Appraisal Device

Costs for control purposes are prepared (1) before the fact (in the form of standard, or budgets) and (2) after the fact (in the form of performance reports). Actually, control can be achieved only before the fact. Nothing that happens after the fact can in any way alter or undo what has already been done. The appraisal process that is based on performance reports is useful only insofar as it leads to better performance in the future, by instigating a study to avoid repeating previous mistakes. In addition, knowledge of the fact that an appraisal is to be made can be an important stimulus to good performance on the part of the person being judged. The performance reports used in the appraisal process are both a device for motivating individuals and a means of conveying information to management useful in starting a new planning cycle.

Some concepts underlying the construction of a cost reporting system are:

1. The concept of a standard. Costs can be set forth as a standard against which actual performance is to be measured. A standard cost is a statement of expected costs, or what costs should be under an assumed set of conditions. There are various types of standards. Normally they are predetermined costs and serve both the communication and motivation control functions. They may be expressed as average product costs and as functional or area of responsibility costs in such forms as "normal capacity" costs, "ideal" costs, "current attainable" costs, and "budgeted" costs. When the standard is in terms of specific responsibilities within the firm, it may be classified in varying degrees of detail depending upon the degree of control management desires to exercise. For close control a detailed classification is appropriate so that variations of all types are reportable to management. If close control is not desired, in order to encourage employee initiative, or if not possible, because of the nature of the activity, a broad classification of standards covering longer periods of time or broader area of activity, is appropriate.

2. The equity concept. The person being appraised should understand the basis on which performance is being judged and accept it as an equitable base.

3. The exception concept. Effective reports ordinarily are designed so that attention is focused on areas where performance costs differ significantly from standards.

4. The frequency with which costs are reported depends on the time interval within which significant departures from standards may occur, the cost of reporting, and on the time required to take corrective action.

While the foregoing comments are primarily applicable to subdivisions of the enterprise, there is a quantitative measure especially useful in appraising overall performance of the organization. This measure is the rate of return on investment. The standard against which the return may be compared is the rate of return which might have been earned if the investment were in another enterprise of comparable risk. This is often approximated by the return earned by other companies in the same industry or by other divisions in the same company.

From the foregoing, it should be apparent that no objective, universal definitions can be made for costs used for control. Since costs are constructed in accordance with the motivation desired, they are necessarily subjective, and it follows that "objective truth" has no relevance as a concept in the area of control. This does not imply intentional dishonesty or trickery, any more than do the principles of semantics. It does mean that there cannot be a single, objective definition of costs for control purposes.

HISTORICAL COST REPORTS FOR PLANNING AND CONTROL

The previous sections on planning and control have set forth basic concepts appropriate for cost reports for management. The implementation of these concepts in cost reports rests on varying degrees of reliability. As a result, many firms use the data available in the conventional accounting system as a basis for planning and control decisions. It is appropriate therefore that a statement be prepared indicative of the concepts underlying such cost reports for planning and control. It must be recognized that these concepts are approximations of the more basic concepts previously set forth. In this statement, only those concepts at variance with or supplementary to the concepts underlying corporate reports to stockholder are presented.

1. Assets, exclusive of cash and direct claims to cash, are bundles of services and cost accounting is concerned with the acquisition, utilization, and disposition of services.
2. Acquisition cost is the cash or cash equivalent released, on the acquisition date, to acquire services but there is no reason to assume that every service has an acquisition cost attached to it.
   a. Normally, interest is not recorded as a cost of non-monetary services acquired but is treated separately as a cost of money. This should not preclude the treatment of minor elements of interest as cost when its separation is difficult and involved.
   b. For some purposes (such as a status report on firm investments as an aid in future planning) recognition in memorandum accounts may be granted services to be acquired on the date the order is placed. For most purposes, however, recognition in accounting records may be delayed until the acquisition of the services.
   c. Services acquired should be classified in a manner which facilitates their tracing on subsequent use. Because management normally plans in terms of types of physical units and changes these plans frequently, the most useful basic classification is in accordance with the form containing the services. Other classifications may supplement this basic classification to reveal intended use and assigned responsibility.
3. Utilization Cost is a measure of the cost of the services used in a specific period of time. There are two aspects of this problem: (1) measuring the services used, and (2) assigning a cost to the services used.
   a. In measuring the services used, the following classification is often helpful:
      (1) The services expiring due to the passage of time alone.
      (2) The services which would have been consumed by the passage of time, but were in fact used in the operation process.
      (3) The services used solely because of the operation process.
      (4) The services which preclude reasonable determination of the time of their use and must be treated conventionally, such as types of advertising.
   b. The services used in any period of time should be measured first in terms of a portion of the acquisition cost (according to some assumed flow) to the firm. Ideally, such a measure should reflect the intent of management. For example, if a higher price were paid for some of the services in an asset (as might be the case in the first year's services of a machine or building), the measures of the services used should reflect such managerial intent. If specific intent is not known either by management or the accountant, it seems desirable to reflect the typical use of asset services and measure them in the following manner.
      (1) Services used as acquired (such as labor and utilities) but paid for at regular intervals may be costed as though every service had the same cost within the pay period. This should not however, preclude the more accurate procedure of costing according to individual measures of services used when the amount involved is important or significant and the information is available, as is the case of labor under piece rate pay.
      (2) Services which attach to physical units and flow with them (such as materials and supplies) may be costed at the average cost of each unit in individual bundle purchases or at the average cost of each unit for all bundle purchases in a period of time. When a different average is computed for each bundle purchase, any flow of sequence in which the bundles are used may be assumed. Consistent use of one adopted flow be-

comes important if management is to understand resulting reports.

(3) Services which flow from physical units without any flow of physical units (such as depreciation) may be costed on the assumption that services flow with output and cost assigned as an equal amount per unit of output. Or, the assumption may be made that services flow with the passage of time and services used may then be costed to periods of time either in equal amounts per unit of time or according to some other method of apportionment.

(4) Services whose time of utilization is difficult to determine, such as advertising and administrative salaries, ideally should be set up as assets acquired and treated as utilization cost on some reasonable basis representative of the effort applied through the use of such services. This basic conception, however, should not preclude the general view that such services are used as acquired provided there is no basis for the more satisfactory treatment.

c. In addition to the measurement of services used in terms of acquisition cost, it is sometimes helpful to measure the use of these services in terms of replacement cost[5] so as to provide a separation of the gain or loss due to non-operational factors from the operating gain or loss.

(1) It may be useful to separate general price level gains or losses from specific price level gains or losses.

(2) As services acquired at no cost or at significantly less than fair market value are used they may be measured in terms of replacement cost and the resulting gain separated from other gains.

4. Activity cost is a measure of the cost of the services used in performing some function, such as creating a product or some activity in the process of doing so. Any allocation of costs involves approximations. When allocations are to be made, such as for product costing, they may be measured in terms of utilization costs and may be separated between those due exclusively to the operating process and those which would have been consumed with the passage of time if not used. In some cases it may be possible to allocate services used in a period of time according to one overall basis. In other cases each element of cost may be assigned according to some physical unit representative of the flow of the services. In still other cases where there is no feasible way of allocating costs according to the flow of services, any reasonable basis of allocation may be used.[6]

5. Disposition costs are a measure of the services disposed of during a period of time and are useful in income reports to management. Frequently it is desirable to separate such costs between those whose services were originally used solely because of the operating activity from those whose services were related to the passage of time. Normally they are measured in terms of acquisition costs, but it is sometimes desirable to separate acquisition costs into the two elements of utilization costs and variations of utilization costs from acquisition costs.

a. The cost of services traced to units of products should not be considered disposed of until the product is sold or otherwise relinquished.

b. Services used in operations but not assigned to products should be separately classified in income reports unless there are reasons to defer them. Such reasons relate to the intent of management at the time of their use and the extent to which they are expected to aid in providing revenue in subsequent periods.

COSTS FOR EXTERNAL PURPOSES

Financial Statements

Costs are, of course, an important consideration in the measurement of income and in the valuation of assets for purposes of financial statements prepared for stockholders and other outside parties. Cost concepts relevant for these purposes are included in the statements on "Concepts and Standards Underlying Corporate Financial

[5] Replacement cost is used here as the cash or cash equivalent currently required to replace the services used, not necessarily the physical unit. Also it is conceived in terms of the normal method of purchasing, which involves bundle purchases of services. Replacement cost is thus a share of the cost of replacing the bundle of services which normally will be purchased. The allocable share should be measured in a manner similar to that used in determining the share of acquisition cost used.

[6] There should be no assumption that only manufacturing overhead should be assigned as a cost of product.

Statements" prepared by the Committee on Accounting Concepts and Standards of the American Accounting Association, and therefore are outside the scope of the work of the present committee.

Cost-Type Contracts

Many contractual agreements specify that payment be made on the basis of cost or of cost plus an allowance for profit. In view of the fact that no generally agreed upon definition of "costs" exists, it is important that the parties to the contract define in considerable detail what they mean by "cost" in the particular situation to which the contract applies.

Even though care is taken in framing this definition, it is unlikely that all problems that will arise can be foreseen. Most of these problems pertain to the treatment of "common costs"; that is, costs that relate partly to the work being done under the contract in question and partly to other work done by the enterprise. A case in point is the occupancy costs of a building in which both work under the contract and other work are being performed during the same time period. When the contract itself does not specify how these costs are to be divided, the division should be made in terms of conventionally accepted accounting procedures. To the extent that conventionally accepted accounting procedure do not provide a solution, the appropriate allocation may be made by references to arbitration or to courts of law.

There seems to be a belief in some quarters that there is, or should be, some scientifically correct way of dividing these costs. This belief is incorrect. Although there are generally recognized customs or conventions that may be helpful in certain areas, none of these has, or can have, the status of scientifically valid rules since common costs are, by definition, not precisely identifiable with one specific contract or project.

Committee on Cost Accounting Concepts and Standards

1955

Robert N. Anthony
James S. Schindler
Edward L. Wallace
Glenn A. Welsch
Norton M. Bedford, Chairman

COST CONCEPTS FOR CONTROL*

ROBERT N. ANTHONY
Professor, Harvard University

THE framework your Cost Concepts Committee used to state concepts relating to control is somewhat unconventional, and some background about our deliberations may help to explain why we finally decided on this framework. Initially, we attacked the problem by examining various types of cost constructions that are used for control purposes, in an attempt to find criteria for determining which of these was, in some sense, the "best." We had lots of possibilities: actual costs, basis standard costs, normal capacity costs, current budgeted costs, ideal standard costs, short-run standard costs, direct costs, attainable costs, systems that prorated all overhead, systems that prorated no overhead, and many more. In the course of our long discussions, one committee member would explain and uphold a technique that he had seen used effectively in some company, and another member would counter with a description of a completely different system that he had observed being used with apparently equal effectiveness in another situation. Although we tried very hard to do so, however, we could find no objective way of generalizing on which type of cost system was "best" for control purposes.

We eventually concluded that an attempt to find objective means of differentiating among the various control systems in current use was not feasible and that our failure to find such criteria indicated that we probably were not approaching the problem properly. The plain fact is that competent managements use a variety of cost constructions for control purposes, and each may find merit in its own system. It is also true that a system that works well in one company may not work at all in another company, even though the two companies have substantially similar control environments. It therefore became apparent that any attempt to define concepts in terms that implied that one of these systems was inherently good and all others inherently poor, or less good, was bound to be fruitless.

This conclusion led us to attack the problem in quite a different manner. We asked ourselves: "What does the control process actually consist of?" Most authorities agree that control, in the sense in which it is used in business management, has to do with the attempts of one person to direct or influence the actions of other persons. This personal, human element in the process came to be the central focus of our thinking.

Although the management control process is often compared with mechanical or electrical control devices, such as the thermostat, such an analogy is apt to be quite misleading. A thermostat reacts to stimuli in a definite, predictable fashion. When the temperature goes down to a certain point, the furnace is turned on; when the temperature rises to a certain point, the furnace is shut off. Human beings, on the other hand, do not behave so predictably; human reactions to a stimulus are much more complicated, and human control systems cannot be so easily or so precisely designed as mechanical or electrical ones. If, for example, my wife tells me the room is too warm, my reac-

* This paper is one of three presented by members of the Committee on Cost Concepts and Standards at the annual meeting of the American Accounting Association, Seattle, August 31, 1956. It relates to the "Tentative Statement of Cost Concepts Underlying Reports for Management Purposes" published in the April, 1956, issue of THE ACCOUNTING REVIEW.

tion may be (and after years of training, usually is) to open a window or to take some other steps to cool it; but, occasionally, I may procrastinate and do nothing, or I may even argue that the room is not too warm anyway.

Thermostats do not argue, they do not procrastinate, they do not resent being told what to do, they do not do what they think is best. In short, they are not human.

A management control system, which does involve human beings—indeed, whose only purpose is to influence the action of human beings—is therefore fundamentally different from mechanical or electrical controls. It follows that our attempt to examine a system in terms of its mechanics—the methods of setting standards, of prorating overhead, and so on—was bound to fail because it missed the main point entirely. And as soon as we considered the management control process as something that basically involved people and the reactions of people, it became evident that there were some useful things that could be said about the role of cost information in this process.

We ended up by grouping the control concepts under three headings, closely related to human reactions and stated in terms of the purposes for which cost information is used in the control process. These are: (1) to communicate information about approved plans, (2) to motivate people, and (3) to report performance.

COMMUNICATION

With respect to the communication of plans, we had in mind primarily the approved budget, which is the end result of the planning process discussed in another section of the Tentative Statement of Cost Concepts. The approved budget is a communication device in that it tells each unit of the organization something about what management expects it to do during the budget period and also shows the unit how its work fits in with the over-all activity of the organization. In addition to the budget, plans and objectives are also communicated by cost standards.

Any means of human communication inevitably raises the problem of semantics. We are all increasingly aware of the fact that the recipient of a communication rarely, if ever, understands precisely what the author intended to say. This is as true with cost information as it is with any other language, and we therefore call attention in our report to the necessity of obtaining common agreement and understanding throughout the organization as to the precise meaning of the budget figures and cost standards used in that company.

MOTIVATION

Our second heading, costs as a motivating device, relates to what is, perhaps, the most important purpose of all; but it is also the most difficult one to state in writing. Let me try an example in an attempt to show how cost constructions can motivate people, that is, how they can influence the actions that people take. I choose, because it concerns all of us who are teachers, the prosaic matter of controlling the costs of mimeographing or other duplicating work. Visualize a school in which the administration recognizes the necessity for having its faculty generate a certain amount of mimeographing work, but which recognizes also that funds available for this and other purposes are not limitless. How can control be exercised over the amount of funds spent for mimeographing and the manner in which the work is done? Of the many ways of solving this problem, I shall mention only enough to indicate how the cost system can help, in various ways, to motivate the people involved.

One possibility is to have no formal control at all. This is a common practice. When a school chooses to follow it, it presumably relies on custom, informal conversations, or perhaps even warnings of one kind or another, to keep the cost of duplicating work from becoming exorbitantly high. The fact that schools that follow this practice do not use costs as a control device in this area, illustrates the point that cost control is by no means the only possible type of control.

Another possibility is to set up a budget for each department or other organizational unit in the school. Perhaps there will be an item in this budget for duplicating work, or alternatively the budget may specify an over-all amount for the total needs of the department, of which duplicating work is but one element. These two types of budgets can motivate the department head quite differently. The first tells him that he is permitted to incur a certain amount of cost for duplicating work, considered by itself; the second tells him that he has certain funds with which to run his department, and it is up to him to decide whether his needs for duplicating work are more important than other possible ways of spending his departmental funds.

Now let us go a step further. How shall we define the "cost" of duplicating work? Shall we charge the department head with the labor cost of the girl in his own department (or a girl in some other department whose services he may borrow) who cuts the stencils? If we do, we remove any incentive for him to use his own or borrowed help, and we shall therefore expect that he will normally send the work to the central duplicating staff, rather than ask his own people to do it. Shall we charge him for the cost of this central staff? If we do not, there is no reason why he should not use it, whether his need is justified or not, and we therefore encourage thoughtless use of its facilities. If we do charge him, we may encourage him to go outside the school for his duplicating work if he can find an outside party who will do it at a lower cost. Perhaps this is what we want him to do. On the other hand, we may prefer that he have the work done inside. If so, maybe we should charge him only for the direct cost of the central staff, which will set up a differential against outside work.

I could introduce many other ramifications, but I hope I have said enough to demonstrate that to the extent that cost constructions are involved in this problem, the decision as to what type of cost should be used is arrived at, not by trying to find the true, objective cost of duplicating—if there is such a thing—but rather by using cost constructions that are calculated to motivate the department head to act as the administration wishes him to act.

The foregoing situation may be somewhat trivial. To show that similar considerations are involved in a factory problem, let us look briefly at the problem of the control of maintenance and repair costs. The maintenance function is that of keeping the buildings and equipment in good operating condition. This is partly the responsibility of the maintenance department, which incurs costs when it makes repairs or does other maintenance work, and it is partly the responsibility of the operating department foremen, who can influence the amount of required maintenance work by the care they give to their equipment.

There are at least a dozen ways in which the costs of the maintenance department can be charged to the several operating departments, and each gives a different "message" to the foremen as to how they should view their responsibility for maintenance. Here are a few of the possibilities and the implications that are likely to be conveyed by each:

Method No. 1: Do not charge any maintenance costs to the operating departments

Message: The operating foreman has no responsibility for maintenance costs. He requests the maintenance department to do the work that he thinks should be done, and the maintenance department has the responsibility for doing it. The maintenance department is implicitly responsible for the condition of the equipment.

Method No. 2: Prorate total maintenance costs to the operating departments on the basis of the number of direct labor hours incurred in each department

Message: Maintenance costs in total are expected to vary proportionately with plant activity. However, the foreman of each department has no direct responsibility for maintenance work, and the maintenance department, as in the first method, has full responsibility. The operating foreman is told his "fair share" of total maintenance costs incurred.

Method No. 3: Charge departments for each job they have done at a prescribed amount for each type of job

Message: The foreman is responsible for situations that create the need for maintenance work, such as machine breakdowns. The maintenance department is responsible for the cost of doing a given maintenance job. The foreman therefore need not be concerned with the efficiency with which the maintenance men work since he will be charged a prescribed amount for each job no matter how much is actually spent in doing the job.

Method No. 4: Charge each department for maintenance work at a prescribed hourly rate for each hour that a maintenance man works in the department

Message: The foreman is responsible both for situations that create the need for maintenance work and for the time taken by the maintenance people to do the work. Presumably, he has some control over the work of the maintenance men. He may, in some situations, even be authorized to hire outside maintenance people if he believes that they will do the work less expensively than the rates charged by the maintenance department.

None of the above methods is necessarily better than the others. Depending on what management wishes to accomplish, any one of these methods, or other methods not listed, or some combination of them, may be best for a given company. The problem is to decide what direction the motivation should take and then to select a method that influences the foremen to act in this manner.

In essence, the Committee concluded that the method of constructing costs for control purposes is governed by management policy, that the costs system should be designed to help carry out that policy, and that rigid mechanical rules are therefore not applicable.

So far, I have discussed only the basic idea of motivation. Our statement of cost concepts ideally should go considerably beyond this basic idea and list specific points that can be used as guides in constructing costs used for control purposes.

Frankly, we have made only a small beginning in this direction. We do emphasize the necessity for relating costs to personal responsibility, which is the "responsibility center" or "activity center" concept that has been written about extensively in recent years. We attempt to be fairly specific about what, as a practical matter, is meant by personal responsibility since there are few, if any, cost elements that are completely and solely the responsibility of a single person. But we do not feel sure enough of our ground to make very many generalizations in this area. The topic is one which is of great concern to people in practice, but it is also one on which, for some reason, not much has yet been written. We therefore simply cannot find many points that are sufficiently well substantiated to warrant including them in the Tentative Statement. This is one of the areas in which our statement is indeed extremely tentative, and with the passage of time, I think many specific and useful points can be added to this section of the statement.

Before leaving this subject, I want to mention briefly two other points that trouble some with whom we have discussed this section of the Tentative Statement.

One is the fact that people being the way they are, not everyone is motivated identically by the same stimulus. That this is so, is undeniable. Nevertheless, there must be some common patterns of human behavior that apply to large numbers of people. To go back to the example of the faculty members and the duplicating work, there undoubtedly are some faculty members who will not order too much duplicating work no matter how much leeway they are given, and there probably are some who will, in one way or another, obtain too much no matter how tight the control system is. But these groups must constitute only a minority, for if most people were in the first group, controls would be unnecessary; and if most were in the second group, controls would be impossible.

The second point is that to some people the very attempt to describe costs in terms of human reactions smacks of trickery, of attempting to fool people. I think this feeling arises from the implicit assumption that there must be some objective way of defining cost, and as we emphasize in the introductory section of the Tentative Statement, this simply is not so. Perhaps it is sufficient to say here that any attempt to use costs to trick or mislead the organization is likely to be self-defeating, in that it will motivate people in quite a different direction from what is intended.

REPORTING

We come now to the third area, costs as a basis for reporting and appraising performance. In this area, we first must face a familiar paradox, which can be stated as follows: Cost reports describe what has already happened; therefore they cannot be used to control events, since no one can alter or undo what has already been done; therefore, a control report cannot really control anything.

One explanation of this apparent paradox is obvious, namely, that cost reports provide the basis for actions such as praise, criticism, or suggestions for change, all designed to improve *future* performance. We think, in addition, there is another, more subtle way in which cost reports influence performance, and indeed influence the very performance being reported on. Advance knowledge of the fact that a report on performance is going to be prepared can be an important stimulus to good performance on the part of the person being judged. I think this is well illustrated by our process of grading students, for it is doubtful that we would willingly undertake the grading drudgery unless we believed that the fact that students knew they were eventually going to be graded had in some way influenced the work they did during the year.

In the Tentative Statement, we list some concepts that are relevant to the reporting area, including methods of constructing and using standard costs, the idea of management by exception, the important point that control systems are likely to be ineffective unless the people involved believe that the standards are reasonable and equitable, the use of return on investment as an over-all yardstick of performance, and so on. I think these are adequately stated in the report, and I will therefore not elaborate on them here.

CONCLUSION

This, then, was our approach to enumerating and defining the concepts relevant to costs for control. Our framework was the *purpose* for which costs are used. In such a framework, we recognized that human reactions and motivations were dominant considerations. Our problem thereupon became not strictly an accounting problem, such as the construction of a set of financial statements, nor an accounting-economics problem, such as that discussed in the planning section of the Tentative Statement. Rather, it was a problem involving both accounting and psychology, the study that deals with human reactions.

Your committee is not made up of psychologists; in fact, its members are somewhat skeptical of some of the psychological patter. We are convinced, however, that approaching the control problem in terms of human motivation—subjective though this approach is, and different though it may seem from the customary language of debit and credit—is much more fruitful than an attempt to define "true" costs, or to say whether ideal standards are better than normal standards, or any other mechanical approach.

The usefulness of such an approach becomes apparent when the concepts are applied to a practical control problem. Without such an approach, one can easily become immersed in pointless arguments on such matters as whether rent should be allocated on the basis of square footage or cubic footage. There is no sound way of settling such disputes. With the notion of motivation, the problem comes into clear focus: What cost constructions are most likely to induce people to take the action that management desires? Answering this question in a specific situation is difficult, and very little in the way of guides toward a specific answer will be found in our statement. But, at least, we think the concepts suggested here describe what the accountant is trying to do.

And as time goes on, we expect that out of experience, and discussions like the one we have today, more specific statements will evolve, so that eventually principles will be developed in the control area comparable with those developed over the years in the financial accounting area.

Behavioral Science and Accounting Research

DAVID O. GREEN*

If inability to complete a task is some measure of its difficulty, then my assignment, to review *Accounting and Its Behavioral Implications* edited by Bruns and DeCoster, can only be regarded as impossible.[1] Selwyn W. Becker, my colleague at the University of Chicago, helped to write this paper. Some of the paragraphs that follow are his, some are ours and some are mine; where it seems important, I shall try to designate authorship.

With their first two words, Bruns and DeCoster have dealt us a low blow. These two words are "behavioral accounting." A neologism, a barbarism; yet I fear their coinage will succeed. If unbearable repetition will foster success, I am confident it will succeed. Bruns and DeCoster provide the usual preface and a prefatory note to introduce each of the five major parts of the collection. These six items contribute only some seven full pages of text yet they contain thirty-three uses of the term, behavioral accounting. Eight times on page 4! Curiously, the two-word term is not employed in any of the 40 collected items. More curiously, it is not defined by the neologists. Unfortunately, and sad to say,

* David O. Green is Professor of Accounting at the University of Chicago.

[1] William J. Bruns, Jr., and Don T. DeCoster, eds., *Accounting and Its Behavioral Implications* (New York: McGraw-Hill Book Co., 1969).

it seems to derive from Becker's conference put on about "you, the new behavioral accounting scientists."[3]

The reason for this molehill expansion about terminology should become clear as we try to define the term.

DEFINITION OF BEHAVIORAL ACCOUNTING

Before examining Bruns and DeCoster, we present a taxonomy of behavioral accounting research in general. Behavioral accounting deals with the behavior of four groups of people: (1) subjects whose behavior provide data for accounting reports, (2) company accountants who process the data, (3) public accountants, and (4) recipients of accounting reports. If accounting reports are categorized as either internal or external, any item of behavioral research should be identifiable as pertaining to one (or more) of the cells shown in exhibit 1.

EXHIBIT 1. CATEGORIES OF BEHAVIORAL ACCOUNTING RESEARCH

	Subjects	Accountants		Recipients
		Company	Public	
Internal				
External				

In addition, to qualify as behavioral accounting research, the explanatory variables being investigated must be noneconomic; that is, economic theory must be inadequate to explain the behavior under investigation. Thus, if the behavior under investigation is that of the subject of an accounting report, of the accountant himself, or of the recipient of an accounting report, if the behavior relates either to an internal or external report, and if the behavior can be better explained by appeal to noneconomic variables, that research qualifies as behavioral accounting research.

WHY EXCLUDE ECONOMICS?

Economics is excluded for two reasons. First, because economics is the mother discipline for accounting theory and has been the social

[3] Selwyn W. Becker, "Discussion of the Effect of Frequency of Feedback on Attitudes and Performance," *Empirical Research in Accounting: Selected Studies 1967,* supplement to Vol. 5, *Journal of Accounting Research,* p. 228. Reprinted in Bruns and DeCoster, p. 420.

science studied most intensively by most accountants (at least, accounting educators) throughout this century, we doubt that it is the fountainhead for the "new" interest. Second, we believe that the "new" interest is in the "behavioral sciences," a term apparently coined at the University of Chicago in the late 1940s by a group of faculty members who used that term because its neutrality made it acceptable to both social and biological scientists.[8] The disciplines that study behavior include "mathematical biology, biochemistry, physiology, genetics, medicine, psychiatry, psychology, sociology, economics, politics, anthropology, history, philosophy, and others; of these, anthropology, psychology, and sociology are the behavioral sciences most examined by business students. Economics, then, remains a discipline outside the so-called behavioral sciences.

Some examples of observed "anthropological" behavior which seem best explained by economic variables follow:

1. The sacred cow complex of North India. It seems best explained by the fact that economic value is maximized through nonslaughter. This is because of the food value of the milk, the fuel value of the dung, and the work value of the beast. After a natural death, the flesh is eaten, if it is not diseased, and the hides are used.
2. Cantonese cuisine — the elaborate prepreparation of thinly sliced ingredients — is attributed to the lack of cooking fuels, a scarce resource when compared with the labor of slicing. As one moves north, the styles change as the fuel supply improves.
3. A tribe of South American Indians — the Nomads of the Long Bow — practice private commensalism and public copulation. Food is the scarce resource.
4. The requirement of clerical celibacy is explained as a device to preclude the dissipation of what would otherwise be the wealth of the church through the laws of inheritance. It did not start this way and has recently been brought into question.

In an accounting context, a switch from FIFO to LIFO is best explained by an economic variable, that is, minimization of the present value of income tax payments. A recent example of observed behavior which cannot be explained with economic variables is the Chrysler Corporation switch from LIFO to FIFO which added $53 million to its tax bill.

[8] Editorial, "Behavioral Science, A New Journal," *Behavioral Science* 1, 1 (January 1956): 2.

Another possible reason for isolating economics is that it is the least conjectural and most rigorous of the social sciences. While not without conflicts and disputes, predictions or forecasts from "opposite" economic theories give rise to differences that seem small compared to the other social sciences. For example, consider the recent furor over the Administration's 1971 Gross National Product forecast of $1.065 trillion when the standard or consensus forecast was $1.050 trillion. Aside from absolute size, the difference must strike most accountants as trivial, certainly immaterial. This suggests that experimental replication is easier in economics and that less replication is required.

SCOPE OF BRUNS AND DeCOSTER

We explained our taxonomy to an above-average M.B.A. student and asked her to read each of the papers in Bruns and DeCoster's collection carefully and then record where, if at all, each would fit.[4] Her findings are reproduced in exhibit 2.

EXHIBIT 2. TAXONOMY OF BRUNS AND DeCOSTER ARTICLES

	Subjects	Accountants	Recipients
Internal	27, 38	9, 10	1, 11, 12, 13, 14, 15, 16, 17, 18, 19, 20, 21, 23, 25, 28, 29, 30, 31, 32, 33, 37
External			22, 26

Notice, on this student's reading, thirteen of the forty papers did not seem to fit our initial specifications of behavioral accounting research; we did not ask that she make the economic/noneconomic variable distinction. This is not to say that in her opinion those that fit were "good" and those that did not fit were "poor." Often the contrary was true. Perhaps other readers would not complete the assignment similarly, yet, Dopuch concluded that sixteen of the forty articles were not related to behavioral accounting research at all.[5]

[4] The table of contents from Bruns and DeCoster is reproduced in Appendix A, pp. 105-07.

[5] N. Dopuch, "Behavioral Science in Accounting," unpublished paper (University of Chicago, 1969).

DOPUCH'S EVALUATION

Interested solely in management accounting research employing psychological concepts, Dopuch further excluded six papers on simulation because psychology was not employed in their hypotheses; two articles were excluded because external accounting issues were primarily involved; and two were excluded because their concern was principally with method.[6] Thus, he found fourteen papers directly related to one of the behavioral sciences and management accounting. Dopuch then classified this residue into three groups:

1. Five a priori arguments on the relationship of budgetary control and evaluation. These are by Sawatsky; Wallace; Becker and Green; Miles and Vergin; and Brummet, Flamholtz, and Pyle.
2. Four a priori arguments concerned with the interaction of behavior and organization design. These authors were Gordon; Golembiewski; Benston; and Rosen and Schneck.
3. Five empirical studies dealing with budgeting and control. These were items authored by Caplan; Bonini; Cook; Churchill et al.; and DeCoster and Fertakis.

BECKER'S EVALUATION

Becker evaluated the known behavioral science-accounting related research early in 1969.[7] Included were many of the fourteen papers discussed by Dopuch and, in addition, some of the simulations. Becker also categorized the research into three groups:[8]

1. Studies dealing with differences in the amount and kind of financial accounting information (accounting outputs) that decision-makers receive.
2. Studies dealing with differences in coding business events (inputs).
3. Studies dealing with managerial accounting.

Becker's criticisms are always provocative, more often than not correct, sometimes unduly harsh, and occasionally wrong. For example, I think he was both unduly harsh and probably wrong in his criticism of Cook's work.[9] The criticism of Cook was wrong because Becker

---

[6] Dopuch's evaluation is reproduced in part in Appendix B, pp. 108-11.

[7] Selwyn W. Becker, "The Behavior of 'Behavioral' Accountants," in *Accounting in Perspective*, eds. R. R. Sterling and W. F. Bentz (Cincinnati: South-western Publishing Co., 1971).

[8] For Becker's evaluation of these studies, divided into his three categories, see Appendix C, pp. 112-15.

[9] See Becker, "Discussion of the Effect of Frequency of Feedback on Attitudes and Performance," in *Accounting*, eds. Bruns and DeCoster, pp. 417-20.

evaluated the work by asking, "Did it contribute to accumulated behavioral science knowledge?" That was the wrong question. Cook employed some psychological concepts in an experimental setting concerned with reactions to accounting reports. It was not her intention to uncover a startling new finding in psychology. I thought it was an interesting and innovative dissertation. Further, I think it exemplifies how, if at all, behavioral science is useful in accounting studies. We look to behavioral science to suggest new ways to examine accounting inquiries and we may look for either concept or method.

As an excellent example of what I have in mind, let me report on such an application by Arthur A. Brown which, to the best of my knowledge, remains unpublished.

AN "ACCOUNTING" APPLICATION OF A CONCEPT BORROWED FROM AN ANTHROPOLOGIST

Arthur A. Brown, Head of Operations Research with Arthur D. Little, acquired *The Silent Language* by Edward T. Hall while browsing in an airport bookstore.[10] (Hall is a Professor of Anthropology at Northwestern University.) Although fascinated by the entire book ("This is one of the most delightful books I ever came across"), Brown was particularly impressed with one of Hall's charts, reproduced as exhibit 3. Brown took Hall's ten primary message systems and his three aspects of human activity and adapted them to budgeting. Budgeting as a cultural phenomenon is the name of Brown's adaptation, and it appears as exhibit 4.

I have used these charts in my classes for the last five years. I'm not sure that they are useful to students, and I am not sure that they represent anything more than gimmicks. Yet Brown's chart remains the best thing I have found to use as a framework for discussing concepts (not techniques) related to budgets.

Note that, in Hall's terminology, "technical" encompasses the material ordinarily included in university work. Brown's chart seems accurate on this score. The accounting or budgeting books and articles have been concerned with the topics in the outer band. In exhibit 4 many of the cells of the inner two bands suggest areas for interaction between accountants and behavioral scientists.

[10] Edward T. Hall, *The Silent Language* (Greenwich, Conn.: Fawcett Publications, Inc., 1964).

EXHIBIT 3.*

The formal (F), informal (I), and technical (T) aspects of human activity.

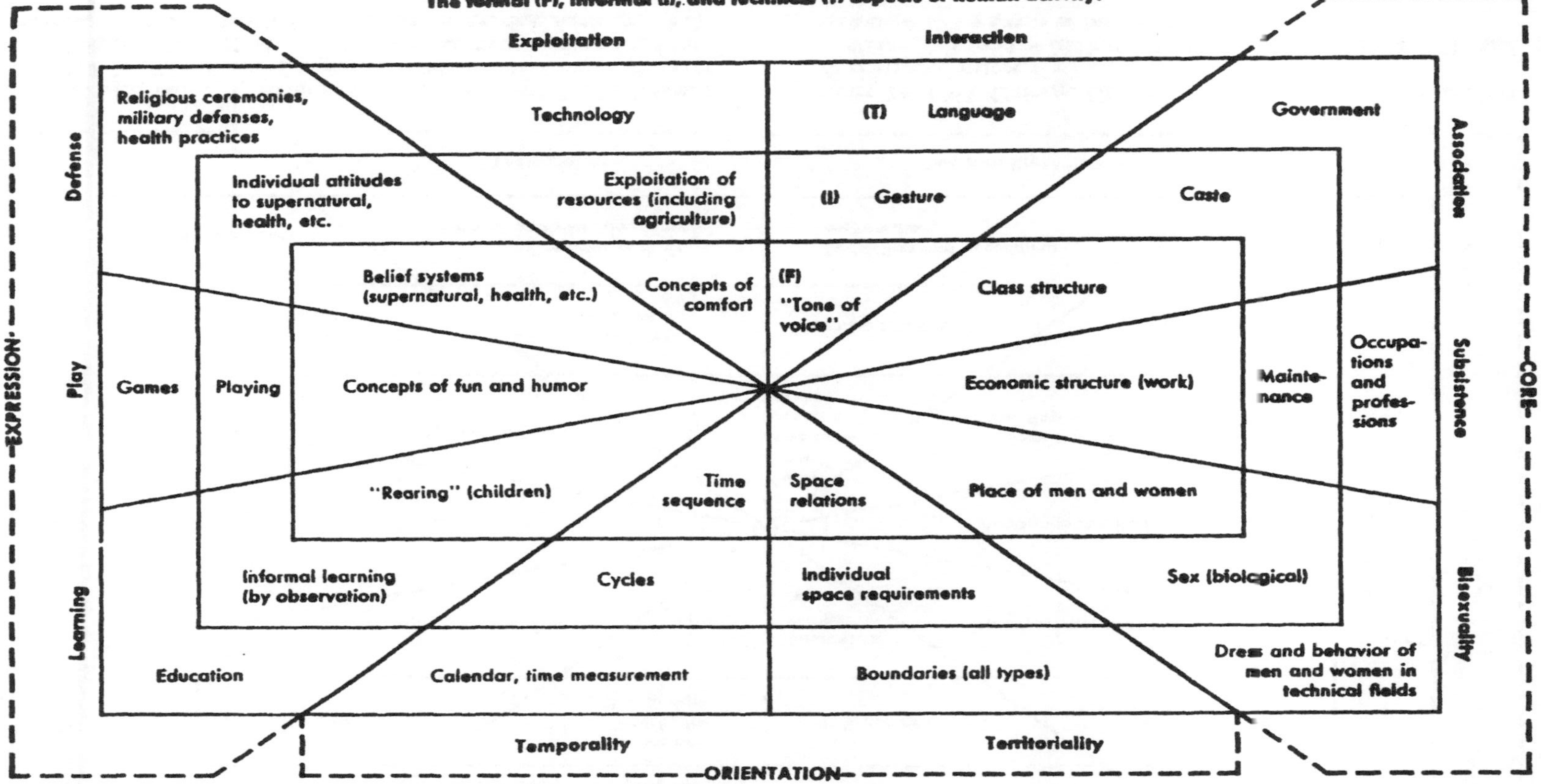

* This diagram is reprinted with the publisher's permission from Edward T. Hall, *The Silent Language* (Greenwich, Conn.: Fawcett Publications, Inc., 1964), p. 92.

Note: T, I, and F indicate the formal (F), informal (I), and technical (T) aspects of human activity. According to Hall, these terms mean:

Formal: Taught by precept and admonition.
Informal: Learned by imitation.
Technical: Transmitted in explicit terms from the teacher to the student.

EXHIBIT 4.†

Budgeting as a Cultural Phenomenon

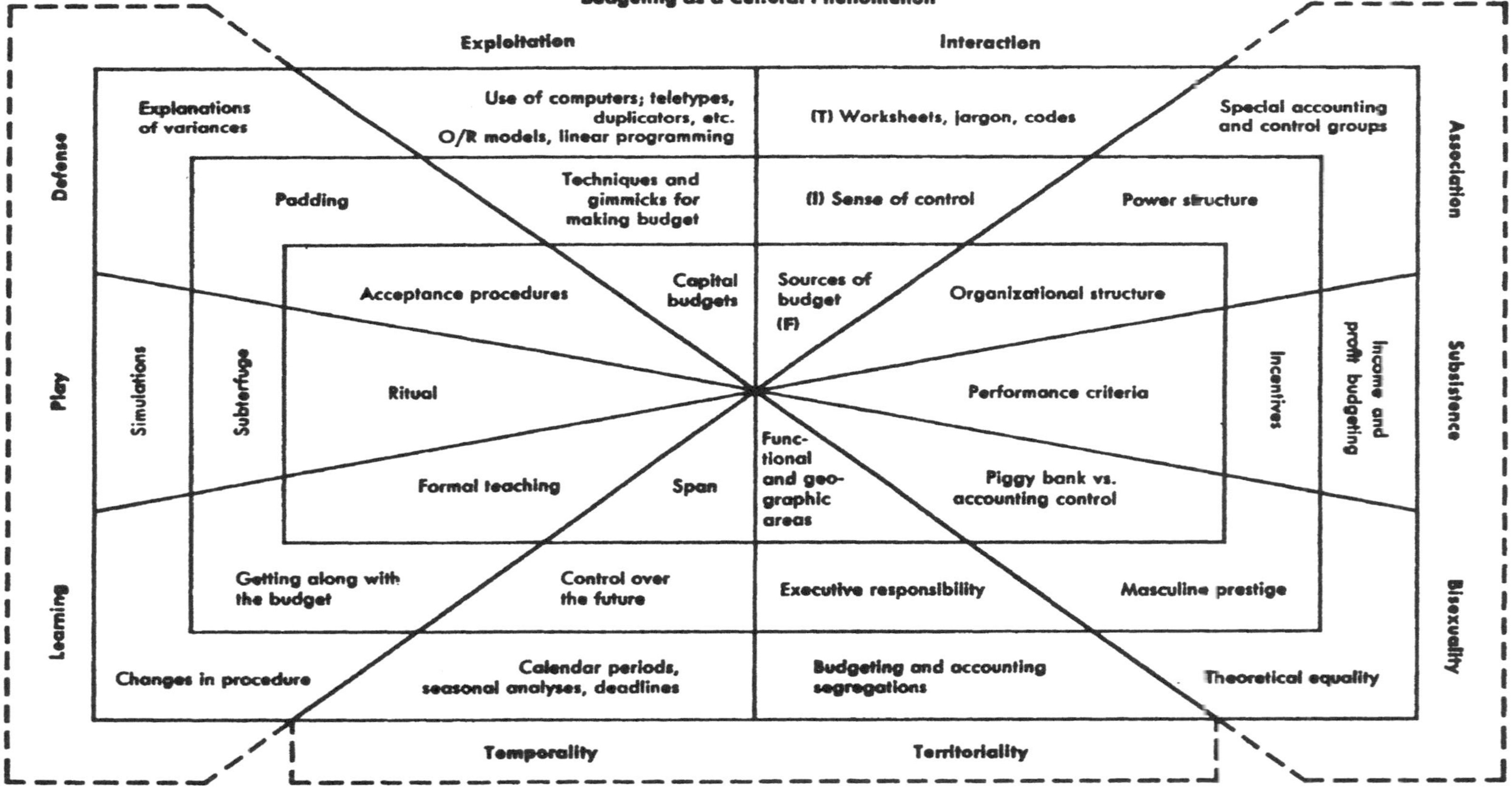

† An adaptation by Arthur A. Brown of an exhibit by Edward T. Hall in *The Silent Language* (Greenwich, Conn.: Fawcett Publications, Inc., 1964), p. 92. This exhibit was presented in a speech, "A Consultant's View of the Budgeting Activity," February 24, 1965, Chicago Chapter, Sixth Annual Seminar, Budget Executives Institute.

Note: T, I, and F indicate the formal (F), informal (I), and technical (T) aspects of human activity.

SOME UNSETTLED ISSUES

In the paragraphs that follow, I would like to consider some issues that were left untouched by Dopuch and Becker. The Bruns and DeCoster collection and other subsequent papers related to the topic tend to suffer from any of one to three great lacks: a lack of historical perspective, a lack of awareness, and a lack of humility or wisdom.

HISTORICAL PERSPECTIVE

Readers, especially young readers, of the Bruns and DeCoster collection are apt to conclude that no accountant ever considered any behavioral science implications before 1960. That is not only unfortunate, it is just not true. I have not combed the literature looking for early examples, but I have found a few items of particular interest. The first, written in 1920, is an antecedent of what is now called responsibility accounting.

> Before the cost accountant then can devise a good cost accounting system, the manager has to perform his prime function, that of organizing properly. It is always possible to make an organization chart of a business which is organized properly and to assign numbers or letters to all the divisions, departments and sections of the organization, using preferably the Dewey Decimal System. Then the accountant steps in and bases his cost system classifications upon the organizational numbers and collects costs by organization units, which enables the manager to hold some one person responsible for each cost-group. This localization of responsibility for costs is the keystone of cost and production control and it the first essential of the sort of cost system expected of the modern manager.
>
> Final costs by articles are, of course, desired, but as far as cost-control and cost-reduction are concerned, final costs are not as important or useful as group costs, that is, responsibility costs.[11]

The May 1916 issue of *The Annals*, The American Academy of Political and Social Science, is devoted to "Personnel and Employment Problems in Industrial Management." There are several items that are antecedents to recent interest in human resource accounting. The following are a few examples. (Pages from which quotes are taken are given in parentheses.)

> This company thinks it economical sometimes to sell slightly below cost, in order to keep its constant labor force. (p. 153)
>
> In five years he cut down the annual labor turn-over from 150 to 33 per cent. He raised average weekly wages by 37 per cent. He reduced working hours

[11] William B. Ferguson, "Relationship of Cost Accounting to Business Management — From the Viewpoint of the Business Executive," *N.A.C.A. Yearbook* (1920), p. 82.

from fifty-four to forty-eight per week. He cut down his average force from 1044 to 865. He increased production 42 per cent. That sort of thing is not charity. It is not sentimental uplift. It comes out in the balance sheet. (pp. 5 and 6)

One machine tool builder . . . looked into the subject with some care and stated it as his belief that the engagement of almost 1,000 persons in his plant during one year, while the permanent increase in his force amounted to less than fifty, reduced his profit by fully $150,000. (p. 135)

Here is one somewhat off the track but interesting.

The budget of the Federal Government should be based upon functions, activities, and projects or what we designate as a "performance budget." Performance budgets focus attention on the work to be done or the service to be performed, rather than upon the things to be acquired such as personal services, supplies, equipment, etc. The all-important thing in budgeting is the work or the service to be accomplished and what that work or service will cost.[12]

One last thought on historical perspective. Bruns and DeCoster passed over at least one item that should have been included and that is the H. A. Simon, et al., *Centralization vs. Decentralization in Organizing the Controller's Department.*[13] This work has been out of print for several years, and it would have been a service to make it available again. Bruns and DeCoster are less able to plead lack of space than most compilers because several items included are not relevant; also they were willing to undertake the task of shortening several items in their collection. For example, article 15 was reduced from fifteen pages to three and one-half.

AWARENESS

What do I mean by lack of awareness? My best examples are not directly from Bruns and DeCoster. Students writing papers on behavioral accounting always seem to find and cite Argyris' article, "Human Problems with Budgets,"[14] but never seem to find Anthony's criticism of it.[15] Even G. H. Hofstede in *The Game of Budget Control* seems

[12] Hoover Commission, *Budgeting and Accounting* (Washington, D.C.: Government Printing Office, 1949), paraphrased from page 8.

[13] H. A. Simon, G. Kozmetsky, and G. Tyndall, *Centralization vs. Decentralization in Organizing the Controller's Department* (New York: The Controllership Foundation, 1954).

[14] Chris Argyris, "Human Problems with Budgets," Harvard Business Review 31 (January-February 1953): 97-110.

[15] Robert N. Anthony, "Distinguishing Good From Not-So-Good Accounting Research," *Proceedings of the 22nd Annual Institute on Accounting* (Columbus: Ohio State University, 1960).

to have overlooked it, although he has a bibliography of over three hundred items.[16] Thus, only one side of the argument is known, and it is, I fear, the wrong side.

Another aspect of this problem is the apparent use of only one source or one authority in making an argument. An example of this is Revsine's "Change in Budget Pressure and Its Impact on Supervisor Behavior" in which he cites only Schroder, Driver, and Streufert, *Human Information Processing* (New York: Holt, 1967).[17] My impression is that there is at least as much controversy in the behavioral sciences as in accounting, and probably more. I have not read Schroder, but Revsine continues the use of two of its items, both coinages, I believe: "eucity" and "noxity." Neither is in *Webster's Third Unabridged Dictionary,* and how many of us have secretaries to explain that eucity derives from the Greek prefix, eu? On this point, I do not know whether to fault Revsine or DeCoster and Fertakis on this lack as Revsine was only trying to help explain the anomalous results reported by DeCoster and Fertakis.[18] (I applaud him for his effort because, although I read it several times, I never understood the DeCoster and Fertakis paper.)

HUMILITY AND WISDOM

The thoughts that follow are occasioned in large part by the Hofstedt and Kinard essay, "A Strategy for Behavioral Accounting Research."[19] Their paper is intended "to help shape future behavioral accounting research," and "... to advocate an overall strategy for approaching future research and a means whereby topics and methods may be selected and then evaluated, both in their own right and relative to existing work."[20] (Do others find this as galling as I?) One of the things I think we accounting teachers have learned, in part, from our behavioral science colleagues is the value of empiricism. Hofstedt and Kinard offer no evidence that an overall research strategy has ever been appropriate or productive. On my evaluation of what has been

---

[16] G. H. Hofstede, *The Game of Budget Control* (New York: Van Nostrum and Company, 1967).

[17] Lawrence Revsine, "Change in Budget Pressure and Its Impact on Supervisor Behavior," *Journal of Accounting Research* 8 (Autumn, 1970): 290-92.

[18] Don DeCoster and John P. Fertakis, "Budget-Induced Pressure and Its Relationship to Supervisory Behavior," *Journal of Accounting Research* 6 (Autumn, 1968): 237-46.

[19] Thomas R. Hofstedt and James C. Kinard, "A Strategy for Behavioral Accounting Research," *The Accounting Review* 45 (January 1970): 38-54.

[20] Ibid., pp. 38-39.

accomplished in the area to date, this is no time for closure. Had I been asked by an accountant a few years ago to state a procedural rule for conducting behavioral accounting research I might have replied, "Get yourself a behavioral science partner." Following this rule did not help Schiff and Lewin avoid the appearance of lack of wisdom.[21] Their study was based on observations of three large corporate divisions. From this they determined that management creates "slack to achieve attainable budgets and to secure resources for furthering their personal goals and desires."[22] They go on to conclude:

> This behavior seems universal among managers; it occurs in profitable and unprofitable companies, whether stable or growing. Our study also suggests that the practice is widespread among controllers who are closely aligned with top management and assume the dominant role in the budget and control process of a decentralized control system.[23]

[21] Michael Schiff and Arie Y. Lewin, "Where Traditional Budgeting Fails," *Financial Executive* 36 (May 1968): 50-52, 55-56, 61-62.
[22] Ibid., p. 62.
[23] Ibid.

Appendix A

Accounting and Its Behavioral Implications
William J. Bruns, Jr. and Don T. DeCoster, Editors
(New York: McGraw-Hill Book Co., 1969)

Contents

Appendix B

Evaluation of Behavioral Research in Accounting

N. DOPUCH*

A PRIORI ARGUMENTS DEALING WITH BUDGETS AND CONTROL

Becker and Green discuss conditions under which participation by workers in the budgetary process may lead to improved efficiency of operations. Improved efficiency may result both because the workers are induced to apply their specialized knowledge to the situation and because they are motivated to internalize the budget as their goals and their standards of performance. As Becker and Green and Stedry indicate, however, the conditions under which participation leads to positive results are a function of both organizational design (autocratic versus democratic) and group and individual psychological concepts (cohesion and aspiration levels). If these hypotheses are correct, then participation may have to be initiated by management since its overall success relies on the managerial prerogative of organizational design and leadership styles. The paper by Wallace also deals with participation, but in a much less rigorous fashion.

Sawatsky discusses Maslow's theory of motivation and on the basis

* The following excerpts are from N. Dopuch, "Behavioral Science in Accounting," unpublished paper (University of Chicago, 1969). Authors and articles reviewed appear in William J. Bruns, Jr. and Don T. DeCoster, *Accounting and Its Behavioral Implications* (McGraw-Hill Book Co., 1969).

of the theory recommends some rather extensive changes in organizational design. Again, we would have to question whether it is an accountant's function to make such kinds of proposals. Miles and Vergin barely touch on psychology and in general try to justify quality control techniques within a behavior-oriented control system. Frankly, I do not think they carry this off. The final paper by Brummet *et al.* is a research proposal based on some of Likert's theories about organizational performance measures. Essentially their proposal requires an explicit recognition of human values within an accounting system of control. Unfortunately how these values are to be measured is not explained. Nevertheless, the proposal has intuitive appeal.

A PRIORI ARGUMENTS RELATED TO ORGANIZATIONAL DESIGN

The paper by Rosen and Schneck which is part of the second group is very similar in content to the Brummet *et al.* paper. That is, Rosen and Schneck also base their paper on Likert's theories. Their main proposal is that behavioral scientists and accountants should do more joint research in an effort to develop measurement systems which incorporate measures of human values. Again, these authors do not offer us guidelines which would allow us to operationalize their proposals.

Benston and Golembiewski discuss the relationship between organizational design and motivation. It is ironic that both of these authors use performance measurement as a basis for recommending two opposing points of view. Benston maintains that performance reports in responsibility accounting permit the implementation of programs of decentralization which, in turn, provide positive contributions to motivation. Golembiewski, however, asserts that an emphasis on performance also within the context of responsibility accounting is a logical outgrowth of a narrow conception of modern organizations. That is, performance measures restrict the usefulness of accounting for broader purposes of control. Regardless of which author is correct, management, not accountants, must determine the organizational design which it feels is appropriate. The accountant must then design his system accordingly, whether this means operating within a democratic or autocratic organization.

The paper by Gordon is consistent with this view since his main concern is how well the accounting system captures the total responsibilities of managers throughout the organization. This seems to be the essence of the behavioral issue in managerial accounting. Given that management has designed its organization either along autocratic or democratic lines, the question is to what extent does the accounting system facilitate the implementation of this design? For example, an autocratic system presupposes the ability to accurately specify standards of performance (accuracy encompasses measurement and conceptual problems) throughout the organizational hierarchy. This is unlikely to be accomplished in the areas of administrative and manufacturing overhead. The main issue then is how do managers and workers react to a control system which includes inaccurate standards? If they react in a dysfunctional manner, then management must either invest in developing more accurate standards or change its organizational design.

A thesis by Anthony Hopwood, University of Chicago, is concerned with this problem, and in particular the conditions under which dysfunctional reactions can be predicted. His assumption is that completely accurate standards can rarely be achieved in firms. He has observed that reaction to this situation varies within the organization, being influenced by such factors, as the importance of accounting data in performance appraisal vis-à-vis other sources of information, the knowledge of managers and workers about the intricacies of accounting, the mobility aspirations of managers, leadership styles and so on. His findings bear on the validity of the empirical studies of Argyris and DeCoster and Fertakis. These authors were concerned with the impact of budget pressure on organizational performance. However, the impact of budget pressure will vary from firm to firm and from department to department depending on the importance of the budget in the firm's planning and control systems. This is not to belittle these studies; rather we must recognize the specific context in which such studies are undertaken.

The results of Cook's study are also related to this point. Cook found that where accounting performance reports were the *only* source of information on performance, increased frequency of reporting led to better results. Her research was based on a business game simulation in which performance reports were the only source of information to the participants. Of course, workers and managers in actual firms have many other sources of information on performance, and different results would probably be obtained if the research were conducted in an actual setting.

I think we must dismiss Bonini's results on a similar basis. As one part of his study, he examined the effects of different accounting measurements (lifo and fifo) given a mathematical decision model. These effects were translated into indexes of pressure which in turn affected the ability of decision makers to achieve lower costs, increased sales, etc. The results of this research are strictly a function of his mathematical model, which has yet to be verified.

Churchill, Cooper, and Sainsbury related some findings concerning the actual and anticipated effects of audits. Their results were not unexpected, but nevertheless they may be useful in managerial control—particularly in the area of managerial audits. If managers' decision processes are evaluated, we can expect these processes to adapt to the standards and goals of the auditors. This is an acceptable outcome of the audit process providing the standards and goals of the auditor are consistent with the long-run success of the organization.

The final paper of the 14 listed earlier is by Caplan. He maintains that present managerial concepts are consistent with the traditional economic concept of the firm. Accepting the Carnegie theory of "satisficing" as a model of present-day organization, he criticizes traditional accounting accordingly. Using a questionnaire, he surveyed five firms and found that the respondents' views confirmed his assumptions about the dominance of traditional theory. Assuming that this is true, it is difficult to infer how we should be concerned about such a result. Does this mean that the modern theory of organizations does not hold? Or does it mean that we should require all participants of the organization to change their views? More important, what are the implications for accounting systems designs if and when managers and accountants change their views about organizations?

This is an appropriate note on which to end this evaluation of the 14 papers since it seems that they all have one thing in common: They raise more questions than they answer.

Appendix C

Evaluation of Behavioral Research in Accounting

SELWYN W. BECKER*

There were seven studies in the first group — 2 by Bruns, 3 by Dyckman, 1 by Jensen, and 1 by Khamakhem. Bruns had subjects play a business game in a laboratory setting in which they made price, advertising, and production decisions. The subjects were divided into 3 groups: one receiving a balance sheet with a LIFO method of inventory valuation, one with FIFO, and one with direct costing. Bruns concluded that the different methods of inventory valuation did not affect decisions. This is not too surprising. Bruns never presented any hypothetical reasons why inventory valuation, which affects reported earnings, should affect the kinds of decisions he asked his subjects to make, and if they should, in what way. Bruns used the same game in a second study wherein he investigated the effects on decisions of receiving an annual report compared with quarterly reports. Again, he stated no theory, no hypothesis, and no differences. The no differences finding could be attributed to the fact that from the statistics necessary to the

* The following is an excerpt from Selwyn Becker, "The Behavior of 'Behavioral' Accountants" in Robert R. Sterling and William F. Bentz (eds.), *Accounting in Perspective: Contributions to Accounting Thought by Other Disciplines* (Cincinnati, Ohio: South-Western Publishing Co., 1971), pp. 70-74. Reprinted with the publisher's permission. Many of the articles discussed appear in William J. Bruns, Jr. and Don T. DeCoster, *Accounting and Its Behavioral Implications* (New York: McGraw-Hill Book Co., 1969).

play of the game, subjects could gain enough information that interim reports added nothing to the decision maker's information. In both studies, there was insufficient experimental control over the factors affecting the dependent variable — the decisions.

Dyckman's first study also was a laboratory situation where subjects were asked to make an investment decision by specifying dollars per share for two firms, one whose inventory was valued on a FIFO basis, and one on a LIFO basis. Subjects were not given information sufficient to adjust for the different methods so the differences in reported earnings produced differences in price per share.

In his second study, Dyckman added operating data to the subjects store of information, and he then found that differences in inventory valuation did not affect decision making. This time, however, his subjects made operating decisions on advertising, production, R & D, price, and dividends rather than an investment decision. Thus it was impossible to determine if the no differences were due to the added information or the different decisions.

Dyckman's third study was designed to answer questions left unanswered by the first two. Subjects were asked to evaluate firms as purchase opportunities and to assign dollar values to each firm. Different methods of valuing inventory made a difference. However, when a small number of subjects were also given operating data, the difference seemed to disappear.

That leaves us in the air not only about the effects of complete information, but also about the effects of inventory valuation because in all his studies Dyckman deliberately confounded size with inventory valuation. In his data analysis, he showed that size alone didn't affect decisions, but because of his choice of statistics, he was unable to test for an interaction effect.

Jensen's study seems to give the answer to this question. He varied depreciation and inventory methods on balance sheets mailed to financial analysts who were asked to make portfolio recommendations. Jensen found all main effects significant and no relevant interaction effects. Jensen speculates that "as in most real world situations, it would have been a hopeless task for an analyst to attempt to try to place the financial reports on a common accounting basis." Presumably, then, we can conclude that when a coding technique changes a number that is *relevant* to a decision, and the decision maker doesn't have enough information to evaluate the coding mechanism, different coding techniques will lead to different decisions. This could have been determined in a single, well controlled experiment.

The final item of research in the "coding effects decisions" category adds nothing to our knowledge. Khamakhem demonstrates that subjects instructed to maximize funds use funds statements more frequently than those instructed to maximize earnings. The latter group more frequently use earnings statements. Some other conclusions were also made about use of funds statements, but since all the conclusions were based on Chi Square Tables with inflated N's, the conclusions, whatever they are, are irrelevant. I mention this research rather than ignore it, because some accountants think highly of it: it was a winning paper in the American Accounting Association's manuscript contest for 1967.

The second category of research includes four studies: two by Archibald, Beaver, Sorter, and Becker; one by Archibald, and one by Neumann. In the first study, on which I collaborated, we found that financial executives' scores on an authoritarianism scale could predict whether the firm used one set of books for tax and another for book purposes. The second study replicated the findings of the first study by using a measure of the intolerance for ambiguity. In addition, we found that the depreciation decisions correlated with the defensive position of the firm as that position was reflected by certain financial ratios.

Archibald investigated changes in depreciation decisions and found some support for the hypothesis that changes were made, at least partly, to smooth income. Neumann investigated auditors' behavior and he found great inconsistencies in their noting of exceptions. Auditors in different offices of the same public accounting firm followed different policies; policies differed within and between industries. In fact, whether or not a change was deemed material seemed to be entirely up to the discretion of the individual auditor.

The third category includes studies by Cook, Stedry, Caplan, Churchill and Cooper, and DeCoster and Fertakis. Since I have commented elsewhere on Cook's and Stedry's papers, I will not repeat myself here. Caplan demonstrates in his study that he is interested in interesting things, but that may be all that he demonstrates. He set out to compare managerial philosophies of 20 management accountants with those of 20 nonaccounting managers. He found no differences. He also wanted to determine the degree to which those philosophies reflected "traditional" or "modern organization theory" assumptions about behavior. He never specified the kind or size of firm from which his sample came. A more serious problem is the kind of measuring instrument he used. He developed a questionnaire which almost precludes finding differences. Except for a few, the wording of the questions almost demands a socially desirable response. In other words, if one were to survey all managers and find out what responses they all thought it desirable to make, or what responses they thought would please stockholders, we would have what we could call a social desirability scale for managerial philosophy. The responses to Caplan's questionnaire look exactly like a social desirability scale. The only relevant observation one can make is that accountants and nonaccountants see the role of management accounting both as a control and motivating device.

Churchill and Cooper addressed themselves to a related portion of this problem: the perceptions people have of the internal audit, the auditors and the audit's perceived effect on behavior. Churchill and Cooper say "almost 75% of the respondents indicated either a neutral or a positive attitude toward the internal auditor and the internal audit." This statement is accurate. It is also accurate to state, based on their own data that 63% of the respondents are neutral or *negative* toward the audit; and 74% are neutral or *negative* toward auditors. Using their data, I can come to an opposite conclusion. Such a contradiction is not too serious since most of their conclusions are based on a 60% response rate from their initially small sample of 66 people. About 40% of the people refused to answer the questions when they felt threatened. The answers they gave, I presume, either are socially desirable or relatively harmless. The more meaningful ones were withheld. With such poor interviewing techniques, no conclusions are possible.

Finally, DeCoster and Fertakis studied budget induced pressure and supervisory behavior. They assume, without documentation or reasoning, that budget induced pressure on the supervisor induces him to behave in an inconsiderate fashion toward his subordinates. They found that budget induced pressure was positively correlated with subordinates ratings of considerateness of supervisors. They then performed some dubious statistical manipulations in an attempt to explain their data. They would have been better advised to discuss the derivation of their hypothesis.

Comments on a Paper by David Green

WILLIAM J. BRUNS, JR.*

GENERAL EVALUATION OF GREEN

Accountants have always been concerned about the effects of their work on behavior. Accounting processes have been developed and are utilized to help individuals and organizations achieve their objectives through the behavior of people. Nevertheless, I am surprised by the prominant mention of behavioral problems in accounting and behavioral research in accounting at this conference. Perhaps this recognition will lead to greater interest in behavioral assumptions employed in the formulation of a priori models and in empirical research (or financial and managerial accounting if you prefer to cut our discipline in another way). If so, maybe we can abandon separate sessions and books on "behavioral" matters and get on with the task of being better accountants.

As David Green has noted, many accountants have raised questions about behavior and have based conclusions on assumptions about the interactions between accountants, accounting systems, accounting data, and decision-makers.[1] The problems facing accountants and decision-makers precipitated the early "pioneering studies" in behavioral ac-

* William J. Bruns, Jr. is a Professor at the Graduate School of Business, Harvard University.

[1] See David O. Green, "Behavioral Science and Accounting Research," pp. 93-115, of this publication.

counting. By 1968, Don DeCoster and I felt we could assemble enough articles and studies concerned with the behavioral aspects of accountants and accounting to interest a publisher in a book that would become a handy source for students and other scholars. The result was *Accounting and Its Behavioral Implications* which Green cited in his paper.[7]

Deciding first to assemble a book of collected work and then making it an attractive commercial proposition for a publisher are not always compatible. As we put the book together, choices were required to keep the size of the book within bounds without abandoning broad coverage. We also wanted the book to have some appeal as a supplementary textbook for undergraduate classes. The overall result of some of these compromises was to weaken the book as a collection of the best research on behavioral accounting between 1960 and 1970.

Some obvious weaknesses follow: (1) The book is not all inclusive. Some good related research was intentionally excluded due to criteria concerned with subject, size of the book, and intended functions. (2) All of the work in the book was completed before 1968. Some good work has been done since. For this reason, the book does not fully cover the decade 1960 to 1970. (3) We had some pedagogical objectives in mind when we decided to include some selections. These purposes have not been recognized by all reviewers. (See, for example, the articles which are not mentioned in the classifications by Green, Dopuch, and Becker.)[8] (4) The book was really meant to be only a sampling, a fact which is clearly spelled out in the first paragraph of the preface to the book.

Admitting these weaknesses, let me try to deal with some of the questions raised by Green in his paper. He is concerned over the use of the term "behavioral accounting." Green claims we have used the term without defining it. He also feels it is not a neutral term. On this issue, I believe we can argue that the term is defined by its usage. While we did not intentionally use the term repeatedly to provide a lexicographer with data for reaching the definition, we believe that one who reads the introductory sections of the book will get a good feeling for what we meant by that term and by our use of it. Green and Becker have contributed greatly by trying to derive a definition for all of us who have used the term without being as precise as we should

[7] William J. Bruns, Jr. and Don T. DeCoster, eds., *Accounting and Its Behavioral Implications* (New York: McGraw-Hill Book Co., 1969).

[8] See Green, "Behavioral Science," pp. 93-104, for evaluations by Green, Dopuch, and Becker. For a list of the articles in Bruns and DeCoster, see Appendix A in Green.

have been. If Green meant to discourage the use of the term behavioral accounting, I feel his paper is likely to do just the opposite. By using it as he has, he has given it even greater legitimacy.

Professor Dopuch, in evaluating the content of the book with respect to its relationship to managerial accounting research, seems to have correctly classified (as either a priori or empirical) the contributions that survived his elimination process. I believe also that Dopuch correctly concludes that the studies at which he looked raised many more questions than they answered. Rather than regarding this as a failure of the studies, I see it as evidence of the potential of future work. In almost every case, the questions these studies sought to answer were new questions, and the fact that preliminary research led to an expansion of areas of interest rather than to closure is quite important.

With respect to Becker's evaluation, there is little that I believe I should say here. These thoughts were presented in essentially the same form at the University of Kansas in 1969. I was a discussant of that paper and my critique has now been published.[4] I feel that Becker was unduly harsh; judgments must be made carefully, for this was and is exploratory research. Furthermore, one measure of the success of earlier research is the degree of interest which it has aroused among students and scholars.

Another noteworthy part of Green's paper is his recognition that behavioral accounting is a subfield of accounting. Many critics have overlooked the fact that behavioral accounting is not separate from that which many of us have always done. In his paper, Green says quite explicitly, "We look to behavioral science to suggest new ways to examine accounting inquiries."[5] This conclusion is quite similar to that which we stated in somewhat less succinct form in *Accounting and Its Behavioral Implications*:

> It is essential to recognize that behavioral accounting is actually a sub-field related to the whole range of activities that are identified in management practice as accounting. When we consider sub-classifications of behavioral accounting, we are, in fact, recognizing the variety of the behavioral sciences and the variety of exploratory methods employed in them. The behavioral sciences themselves have generated many questions which remain at least partially unresolved and it would not be difficult to view behavioral accounting as a sub-field of the behavioral sciences. It must not be so regarded,

[4] William J. Bruns, Jr., "The Behavior of 'Behavioral' Accountants: Critique," in *Accounting in Perspective: Contributions to Accounting Thought by Other Disciplines,* eds. Robert R. Sterling and William F. Bentz (Cincinnati, Ohio: South-Western Publishing Co., 1971), pp. 79-83.

[5] Green, "Behavioral Science," p. 98.

however, because the primary consideration of this book, as of those involved in the study of behavioral accounting, is on improving the use of accounting by the use of research tools and knowledge of the behavioral scientist.[6]

Green's comments about the historical perspective of behavioral accounting are appropriately taken. The questions we have raised are not new. It is, instead, the tools and methods that are new. Green is concerned that readers of Bruns and DeCoster may not realize this, but I hope not too many overlook the fact that we began the preface by saying:

Behavioral accounting is a new area of interest and study within the much broader field of accounting, though the questions that provide the focus for behavioral accounting are not new. Thoughtful men have long been concerned about them. We call the field "new" because of the tremendous growth of work and interest, particularly systematic research, in it during the last decade.

The same theme also appears in the introduction to the first part of the book.[7] Green's comments about the need for awareness, humility, and wisdom are valid; yet, I do not know how we can ensure that we or our students are aware and wise.

Green has aptly referred to the faddish aspects of behavioral accounting. I have thought seriously about this aspect. A student once asked me how long I thought the behavioral accounting fad would last. I was taken aback, because I had never thought of behavioral accounting research as being faddish. This student pointed out that many times a movement like behavioral accounting flounders because those who practice do not become involved and those who profess fall victim to unexpected pitfalls in the development of their research effort and program. As a result of this encounter, I looked again at the promises which behavioral accounting presents. In addition, I tried to look at some of the pitfalls which impede progress in this area. I would like to share some of my thoughts with you.

PROMISES FROM BEHAVIORAL ACCOUNTING[8]

Greater knowledge about the way in which accounting processes, systems, and information are used, and about the ways in which the accountant can help the organization and individuals to achieve their

[6] Bruns and DeCoster, *Accounting*, p. 4.

[7] Ibid., p. 3.

[8] Some of the thoughts which follow were discussed in the Accounting Colloquium at the University of Texas on March 19, 1971. I am grateful for comments from faculty and students who attended.

objectives more effectively, promises much for accountants. In particular, I believe behavioral accounting is essential for (1) continued development of the accounting profession as information specialists; (2) greater involvement by accountants in the resource allocation processes of society and enterprises and organizations; and (3) increased self-fulfillment for accountants through the satisfactions that will stem from knowledgeable contributions which lead to organizational success.

As we learn more about behavioral accounting, the degree to which the accountant can assist members of organizations in allocating effort and resources to achieve given objectives will increase. The accountant can emerge as an information specialist, facilitating the activities and processes of the organization itself. Knowledge about the way in which organization members use information will facilitate reports highlighting critical elements. In some cases, perhaps, the accountant may even be able to propose answers to the who, what, why, how, and when questions about the way in which information should be used.

The promise of greater involvement in resource allocation depends upon an increase in accountants' efforts to develop systems which provide and utilize information more effectively. In many cases now, because we do not know who needs information or how it will be utilized, the accountant's work is regarded as complete at the time measurements are made and reported. If we knew more about the processes which are intimately related to accounting (planning, choosing, controlling), the accountant himself could become involved in the development of organizations which would provide for more effective use of resources and greater satisfactions for their members. Working with other elements within an organization or system, the accountant could become more intimately involved with programs for attainment of organization goals.[9]

[9] As an aside, while I was considering these promises, I read the text of Charles T. Horngren's speech to the 1970 Annual Meeting of the American Accounting Association, "The Accounting Discipline in 1999," *The Accounting Review* (January 1971): 1-11. Though he refers to the pace of change (p. 1), I feel the picture of the future which he painted was far too similar to the picture of today. I believe we cannot assume accounting and accountants will be allowed to move slowly while others move fast. Achievement of the first two promises may be the only way accountants can survive.

As an analogy, consider another profession — barbers. Until the sixteenth century barbers were surgeons. During the reign of Henry VIII, an act forbidding barbers to perform any surgery except bloodletting and tooth drawing was passed. Was this because barbers had failed to change as new knowledge of the human body, disease, and health was discovered? In time, barbers lost their right to let blood and pull teeth as well, and a look around some college cam-

In the third promise, I have tried to capture the essence of a subtle increase in self-satisfaction which I believe greater knowledge about behavioral accounting will provide. At the present time most accountants "know" the importance of their work to the organizations or individuals who "need" it. On the other hand, most are unsure exactly how the products of their work are used or the relationship between their work and the on-going activities of the organization. If we learn more about the interaction between the products of the accountant's work and the processes and achievements of organizations, it seems likely that we can increase the level of intrapersonal satisfaction that the accountant obtains by participating in the processes of the organizations and with those individuals with whom he works.

There will be some, I am sure, who feel that these promises are too grandiose and beyond the reach of any accountant, whether he is armed with knowledge from behavioral accounting or not. They will say that an accountant is an accountant, and he will always be an accountant; they will be unable to attribute anything more than is contained in their preconceived image. By contrast, I feel that as the accountant learns to do more and to do it more effectively, he will be asked to do more, and his role in organizations and in society will increase proportionately.

PITFALLS OF BEHAVIORAL ACCOUNTING

While promises of behavioral accounting may be beyond our immediate grasp, the pitfalls are already at hand. Unless we can successfully avoid several obvious pitfalls, work in behavioral accounting may never proceed to the point where the results obtained will allow us to enjoy the fruits represented by the promises.

Specifically, I want to identify four pitfalls and then suggest ways in which they might be avoided. The four pitfalls are: (1) unrealistic expectations about results from behavioral accounting research; (2) failure

---

puses in 1971 would convince some that their last function, hair cutting, is being seriously challenged by a society accenting youth culture.

It would be reassuring to conclude that because barbers lasted five hundred years from the first acts of restriction, accountants can also expect a long existence. But the trend of change in knowledge, technology, and social forms appears to be accelerating very rapidly. See for examples, discussion of the "change revolution" in Neil Postman and Charles Weingartner, *Teaching as a Subversive Activity* (New York: Delacorte Press, 1969), pp. 10-11 and Alvin Toffler, "Part One: The Death of Permanence," *Future Shock* (New York: Random House, 1970), pp. 11-44. If accountants will *not* be doing in 1999 what they are in 1971 (because of changes beyond their control), what will they be doing?

to identify boundaries properly so that too much effort is devoted to insignificant questions or the field is defined so broadly that specific results cannot be obtained; (3) confusion in the focus of attention in areas where results will not be useful; and (4) potential isolation from real-world problems.

UNREALISTIC EXPECTATIONS

The scope of behavioral accounting is extremely broad. It encompasses almost all of what accountants do as well as many considerations which often have been regarded as outside of accounting. This breadth of scope means that the task of developing conclusions from research may be slow and arduous. Behavioral accountants must guard against drawing premature conclusions from inadequate evidence, or they will undoubtedly discover that the support they need quickly evaporates.

Expectations of quick results can come in several different forms. Using my own work as an example, I can recall how at one point I was confident that I would be able to ascertain the way in which individual decision-makers used information about inventory values in making decisions within the business firm. Other researchers also set out to try to study the way in which managers of a particular kind of firm use other types of accounting data. Some reflective critics have suggested that it is unlikely that we will ever know how an individual user or class of users will use an individual kind of data or accounting report.[10] They argue that even if we were able to predict what an average user is, or the way in which an average user would use information provided by the accountant, that finding might not be of much use to us. I am convinced that there is no such thing as an average user, and it is probably futile to try to predict a specific individual's behavior.

Unrealistic expectations already exist regarding the potential contribution of behavioral sciences to accounting problems. Currently, the Accounting Principles Board has distributed for exposure a draft of an *Opinion* dealing with accounting changes.[11] The criteria used in this exposure draft emphasize users. I suspect that this orientation has been partly induced by the direction which we have taken in education over

[10] See, for example, Selwyn Becker, "Discussion of the Effect of Frequency of Feedback on Attitudes and Performance," in *Empirical Research in Accounting: Selected Studies, 1967,* Supplement to *The Journal of Accounting Research* 5(1967): 225-28.

[11] The exposure draft discussed here was revised before being issued as Accounting Principles Board, *Opinion No. 20, Accounting Changes* (American Institute of Certified Public Accountants, 1971).

the last several years. However, it provides ample evidence that at least some members of the Accounting Principles Board think we can do things that are clearly beyond our grasp. Let me quote from the exposure draft:

> The Board concludes that an entity should initially adopt those accounting principles on which the basis of the substance of the facts and circumstances then existing appear to furnish results most useful to financial statement users.

Since we are so often unsure who users are, it is hard to know what "facts" are considered.

Again, quoting from the exposure draft:

> The presumption that an entity should not change an accounting principle may be overcome only if the enterprise demonstrates that an alternative accounting principle that is generally accepted will provide more useful financial information.

This is an example of unrealistic expectations. If our research in behavioral accounting is an example, there are going to be very few accounting changes, because the dominant finding thus far has been that alternative methods do not make much difference in the kinds of decisions people make. Hence, one could be led to the conclusion that alternative methods never provide more useful information.[12]

Many practicing accountants feel great pressure today for changes in accounting principles and standards. It is tempting to suggest that behavioral accounting might provide evidence which would help improve accounting practice through consideration of the relative utility of new classes of information. However, this temptation must be resisted. As much as we might feel that one method as opposed to another is behaviorally more sound, until we have taken the time to develop our knowledge carefully, it would be a mistake to base decisions upon such feelings.

UNIDENTIFIED BOUNDARIES

Because the scope of behavioral accounting is necessarily quite broad, accountants should generally agree upon areas of interest and work should be focused toward the promises set forth above. The accountant must not try to become a psychologist or sociologist, but neither can he narrow his focus of attention to the extent that he does not consider all the variables that are subject to his influence and control. Undoubtedly

[12] In this *Opinion* the criterion for a change in principle was softened to require only that the new principle is "preferable." Whether preferability will be easier to demonstrate than usefulness remains to be seen.

the question of how broadly behavioral accounting should be defined will have to be solved on an ad hoc basis by each researcher.

DIFFUSED FOCUS

In discussing the pitfall of unrealistic expectations above, I alluded to the problem of focus. There is potential danger that we will conduct a plethora of small studies dealing with small questions but fail to develop an adequate general theory that allows us to integrate those findings. We must carefully seek results from which we can generalize to avoid the potential trap of learning more and more about things which are increasingly insignificant. This pitfall is especially dangerous because of the tendency to focus on that which we already know or on those things which seem temptingly like prior work in other behavioral sciences.[13]

ISOLATION FROM THE REAL WORLD

Perhaps the most dangerous pitfall of all is that almost all work in behavioral accounting to date has been done by academic people in an academic setting. In that environment we can study ourselves to extinction and not learn very much that will be helpful. If behavioral accounting is to make a contribution, it must do so in the social and organizational context in which activities take place. At the earliest time possible, therefore, it seems essential to involve ourselves in using the real world as a place for observations and as a laboratory for experimenting with the effects of accounting and its role in social activities, much along the lines Professor Anthony suggests in his paper prepared for this conference.[14]

CONCLUSION

The steps that have already been taken to begin the study of the behavioral implications of accounting are steps in the right direction;

---

[13] The potential problems of relating results in one kind of study (for example, in psychology) to another kind of problem (for example, in accounting) have been well highlighted in exchanges in professional journals. A good example was provided by Fertakis and Jensen. John P. Fertakis, "On Communication, Understanding, and Relevance in Accounting Reporting," *The Accounting Review* (October 1969): 680-91; Robert E. Jensen, "Empirical Evidence from the Behavioral Sciences: Fish Out of Water," *The Accounting Review* (July 1970): 502-508; John P. Fertakis, "Empirical Evidence — A Reply," *The Accounting Review* (July 1970): 509-12.

[14] Robert N. Anthony, "Some Fruitful Directions for Research in Management Accounting," pp. 37-68, of this publication.

some of the pessimistic conclusions Professor Green seems to reach are unwarranted. In the long run, I am confident that the contribution which accounting can make to society will be enhanced if we can learn more about the important interrelationships between data, people, and the organizations and social forms in which we live and work. So long as we move carefully, I am convinced we can make substantial and important progress.

Comments on a Paper by David Green

JACOB G. BIRNBERG*

I would like to divide my discussion of Green's paper[1] into two parts. In the first I will attempt to evaluate his comments as best I can. In the second I will explore in greater depth the conclusion he has reached — that behavioral accounting is a fad that should be encouraged to pass. By dividing the discussion in this fashion, I hope to clarify both the areas of agreement and disagreement.

In reading Green's paper, I detected three main themes. One is the need to delineate the topic under discussion. The second is the need to identify the knowledge gained from the work of behavioral accounting researchers. The third is a plea for a change of emphasis in the behavioral sciences utilized if, despite his advice, we continue to do research in the area.

Green delineated the boundaries of behavioral accounting in two steps. First he defined behavioral science; then he described the nature of the inputs expected from these areas. He determined that behavioral accounting includes those accounting inquiries which derive some element of their approach to accounting problems from anthropology, psychology, and sociology. The relationship could take the form of either methodology or concept(s). His description deliberately elim-

* Jacob G. Birnberg is a Professor of Business Administration at the Graduate School of Business, University of Pittsburgh.

[1] David O. Green, "Behavioral Science and Accounting Research," pp. 93-115, of this publication.

inated two of the behavioral sciences I would have chosen to include: economics and political science. However, some introspection led me to recognize that the facet of political science I consider relevant is describable as political economy. Thus a single issue of relevance is whether to include economics.

The exclusion of economics troubled me at first, for I felt Green could be excluding *economic variables* from those dimensions of the accounting process subject to investigation. However, many of the studies that I technically might have excluded by using his test of inclusion, he himself discussed without reservation. I have in mind papers similar to Bruns' in which economic decision making is examined.[2] Thus, for practical purposes, the scope of the subject matter is adequately defined by Green, and the portion of economics excluded is of its *purer form,* which will cause little difficulty.

Green concluded that relatively little of value has been developed from the efforts of researchers in behavioral accounting. I think that Green, Bruns, and I would agree that at present the literature is in a rudimentary state. If all we have to offer is another ten or twenty years of what we have done up to now (and Bruns and DeCoster is not a bad judgmental sample of research up to about 1967),[3] then we do not promise a great deal for the future. On the other hand, it is probably true that the literature is not as bad as some might portray it to be. For example, Becker is correct when he states that we went through several false starts to get from a problem to its solution.[4] However, two salient points have gone unnoted. One is that these studies not only were concerned with the problem described in the null hypotheses, but they also were testing the acceptability of a new approach to better understanding accounting problems — what we have described as behavioral research in accounting. The second point is the nature of the issue. The accountant would accept as a basic truth Becker's conclusion about the impact of relevant numbers when they are imperfectly coded. The question was is whether inventory was such a relevant number and, if so, if LIFO-FIFO was an instance of poor coding. In addition, if Becker's hypothesis had been tested with a nonaccounting task, at least one more Ph.D. student would have found the basis for one more study using accounting data.

[2] William J. Bruns, Jr., "Inventory Valuation and Management Decisions," in *Accounting and the Behavioral Implications,* eds. William J. Bruns, Jr., and Don T. DeCoster (New York: McGraw-Hill Book Co., 1969), pp. 201-10.

[3] William J. Bruns, Jr., and Don T. DeCoster, eds., *Accounting and Its Behavioral Implications* (New York: McGraw-Hill Book Co., 1969).

[4] See Green, "Behavioral Science," Appendix C.

Finally, Green is correct in stressing the limited scope of our methodology. The issue now as I perceive it is not whether sociology, experimental psychology, or anthropology is better. Rather, stated in the simplest terms, the issue is that we must examine several avenues before deciding which is the most desirable.

As the literature exists today it would appear as if behavioral accounting were a branch of organizational or of social psychology. I can only conjecture as to why this is the case. Perhaps it is caused by the need to be rigorous at a time when rigor is stylish in business schools. In that case laboratory experimentation has the requisite aura of rigor, while sociology may not.

There are, of course, some obvious exceptions to this characterization of the literature. For example, Willingham, Sorenson, and Carmichael have written a variety of papers, all concerned with the applicability of sociological concepts and techniques to accounting problems.[5] Similarly, some accountants have applied the tools of an industrial psychology/personnel approach to assess the satisfaction and professional development of accountants. One such study that has been completed is by Strawser, Ivancevich and Lyon.[6] To the best of my knowledge, Brown (and Green) are in the vanguard in suggesting the significance of anthropology for accountants.[7] This undoubtedly reflects the lack of interest by anthropologists in applying their skills to problems suggesting business applications as much as our lack of awareness of their field.

The greatest portion of my time since receiving Green's paper has been spent reacting to his basic notion that behavioral accounting is a fad that should be permitted — like all fads — to die. In that sense I have had the same somewhat shocked reaction that Bruns had to his student's question.[8] To resolve my own inner anxieties — and to discover if I should begin to plan a new series of interests for the 1970s — I have attempted to make my own evaluation of what the future holds.

Let me begin my assessment of what has happened in behavioral

[5] Typical samples of their work are, D. R. Carmichael, "Behavioral Hypotheses of Internal Control," *The Accounting Review* 45 (April 1970): 235-45; J. E. Sorensen, "Professional and Bureaucratic Organization in the Public Accounting Firm," *The Accounting Review* 42 (July 1967): 553-65; and J. J. Willingham, "Internal Control Evaluation — A Behavioral Approach," *The Internal Auditor* (Summer 1966): 20-26.

[6] R. H. Strawser, J. M. Ivancevich, and H. L. Lyon, "A Note on the Job Satisfaction of Accountants in Large and Small C.P.A. Firms," *Journal of Accounting Research* 7 (Autumn 1969): 339-45.

[7] See Green, "Behavioral Science," pp. 98-100, for discussion of Brown.

[8] William J. Bruns, Jr., "Comments on a Paper by David Green," p. 119 of this publication.

accounting during the 1960s by evaluating where we stand relative to a series of goals. Since this is the behavioral science segment of the program, I will use a somewhat Maslovian hierarchy of goals. Naturally, it will consist of five goals arranged in order of importance. I recognize that the five may contain some overlap and that others could be offered. However, these five are fair statements of the levels of development that any emerging research interest strives to meet.

The first, and the most basic, goal is to establish a legitimate reason for the existence of behavioral research in accounting. Second, having accomplished this, the next level is to adapt or develop the research tools necessary for the researcher to begin the study of the area and to answer simple questions. The third goal is to develop a synthesis of the earlier findings which permits an understanding of more than isolated phenomena and suggests additional areas of research. The fourth level involves the study of more complex phenomena and simultaneously the development of original techniques to analyze the problems of the area. Finally, the fifth and highest need is to develop theories which permit a systematic view of the problem area.

These goals are typical of the ones we could have set when we commenced the study of the behavioral facet of the accounting function (a study that began *in earnest* in the late 1950s and early 1960s). They are representative of the order in which we should strive to develop our understanding. However, they are overlapping in that, as researchers, we may attempt to achieve more than one at any time.

Despite some disagreement, I believe that we have achieved the first goal. Even Green disagrees with Becker's now famous "No Trespass" injunction at the 1967 Empirical Conference. This was to my knowledge the only suggestion that we *could* not research such topics. Of course, there are those who have suggested we *should* not.

The Bruns and DeCoster volume is largely a reflection of our achievement of the second goal.[9] Any one of the articles in their collection reflects the application of existing techniques, usually from experimental psychology, to questions of primary interest to accountants.[10] But in another respect the Bruns and DeCoster volume is a poor indicator of our progress. The organizational psychology bias of the materials con-

---

[9] Bruns and DeCoster, *Accounting and Its Behavioral Implications.*

[10] This is best demonstrated by three articles in Bruns and DeCoster, *Accounting and Its Behavioral Implications*. These are Bruns, "Inventory Valuation," pp. 201-10; Thomas R. Dyckman, "The Effects of Alternative Accounting Techniques on Certain Management Decisions," pp. 211-20; and Abdellatif Khemakhem, "A Simulation of Management-Decision Behavior: 'Funds' and Income," pp. 221-32.

tained in it obscures a fair degree of concurrent progress in the application of sociological concepts to accounting problems. I cited some of these studies earlier.

It is all too clear that in the period covered by the Bruns and DeCoster volume little was achieved regarding the remaining three goals. If anything, the book highlights our failure to integrate our findings and strike out in new and previously uncharted directions. However, it is important to remember that their book, regarded as synonymous with behavioral research in accounting during the 1960s, had a cut-off date significantly ahead of January 1970. Thus a significant portion of research may have been omitted.

What the research in the 1970s will be like is much more difficult to assess. It is safe to assert that a basis has been established so that researchers in the 1970s are likely to have an easier time than those of the 1960s. The question is whether researchers will be able to achieve the third and fourth goals. I believe the answer is yes; I offer as evidence the research that was conducted during the latter part of the 1960s and which was not included in Bruns and DeCoster. If these projects are typical of what we can expect will persist in the next decade, then it is apparent that there is hope.

In general, the greatest weakness I see in the existing literature is that we have not achieved a significant breakthrough in integrating existing findings so as to view more systematically the vast array of existing research (what I before labeled as the third goal). Aside from Ijiri, Jaedicke and Knight, there has been no attempt to achieve this.[11] As a result we lack at least a tentative theory of how accounting information is processed by users. Such a theory once developed would permit the generation of new studies. These studies could explore the implications of the theory and investigate inconsistencies between the model and isolated studies.

What appears to be emerging instead are a series of studies at the second level which are asking more sophisticated questions than those raised by earlier researchers. The works of McDonald and of Sterling and Radosevich typify one group of studies.[12] Such studies begin by establishing a measure of a property that is important to the accounting

[11] Yuji Ijiri, Robert J. Jaedicke, and Kenneth Knight, "The Effects of Accounting Alternatives on Management Decisions," in *Accounting and Its Behavioral Implications*, eds. Bruns and DeCoster, pp. 187-90.

[12] D. L. McDonald, "A Test Application of the Feasibility of Market Based Measures in Accounting," *Journal of Accounting Research* 6 (Spring 1968): 38-49; and R. L. Sterling and R. Radosevich, "A Valuation Experiment," *Journal of Accounting Research* 7 (Spring 1969): 90-95.

reporting process. They then examine the behavior of different measurement approaches in terms of this property. From such studies they can conclude that something is or is not significantly superior to another when rated according to a particular property. Perhaps such studies, vastly superior to the earliest studies on LIFO-FIFO, will encourage others to focus on the issue of how accounting information is processed.

I am aware of only two other studies that may be asking the kind of questions related to stage three. One is a study by Hofsted, who was concerned with whether people, given a stream of numbers, behave differently if they are told that it is an accounting number stream, such as income data, as opposed to bushels of wheat produced in the United States.[13] The answer to this question could save us a lot of work. For example, if people do not differentiate in the way they project the next number in the series, whether it be wheat, a table of random numbers, or accounting data, then indeed we could solve the problem the way Becker did.[14] There would be no need to create all the additional environmental types of material which many feel are necessary.

The second is a study by Haried that attempted to measure the meaning accounting terminology has for various groups.[15] He asked a very interesting question, one to which we must know the answer before we can model the accounting information process. He considered whether the connotations of words may reflect the attitudes of the various parties who receive data toward the entire process of financial disclosure.

The same question might have been considered when the initial pooling versus merger exposure draft came out. There was a great deal of disagreement. Now, the argument might not have been over the question of the possible impact the draft would have but, instead, about basic differences in viewpoints toward disclosure on the part of financial executives, auditors, and readers of financial statements. We could not learn their views by asking them directly, since all kinds of halo effects would exist. However, we might have used the semantic differential to see if significant differences exist in the connotation of financial disclosure to the concerned groups. I apologize for the fact that such a study would be a bit of a fishing expedition, but it strikes me as a fishing expedition that might be worth going on. Perhaps most important is that

---

[13] T. Hofsted in a paper discussed at the Conference on Behavioral Research in Accounting, New Orleans, October 1970.

[14] See Green, "Behavioral Science," Appendix C, for Becker's solution.

[15] A. A. Haried, *An Inquiry in the Semantic Problems of External Communications* (Ph.D. dissertation, University of Illinois at Urbana-Champaign, 1970).

whatever we found now might aid us in the future in assessing *ex ante* the reaction of concerned groups to changes in rules for disclosure or determining how the rules should be developed. Moreover, we would have a more rigorous basis for conjecture other than intuition.

To conclude, if behavioral questions are relevant and if they ought to be investigated, then we cannot rely on organization theorists to ask the relevant question, investigate it, and tell us what the answer is. They have many other things to look at which are more interesting to them and which preoccupy their time. In addition, just as some of their materials are a complete mystery to us, our materials are a mystery to them. Can we expect them to learn accounting in order to research what to them may be a relatively trivial question? If there is a question for which we seek the answer, we will have to find it ourselves.

Discussion Comments — Session 3

Burns and DeCoster were chosen as the focus for the third session of this conference because the studies included in their collection of readings nearly exhausted the population of behavioral science research performed in accounting during the 1960s and thus provided a convenient basis for discussion.

Several participants took issue with Green's pessimistic appraisal of the contribution of behavioral science research in accounting. It was pointed out that because accountants have only recently begun examining behavioral issues, we should expect such research to be rudimentary and mostly exploratory. Moreover the tools are new and the accounting users of these tools are too inexperienced to generate practical results immediately.

It was also noted that accounting reports and control devices inherently contain assumptions concerning user response and human behavior. If these assumptions are incorrect, then the theories and practices which rely upon them are suspect. Thus, the methodology of behavioral research should be used to investigate these behavioral assumptions. If we dismiss the need for such research, we may be perpetuating a reliance on potentially erroneous normative theories.

This point was elaborated on within the specific context of budgeting. If a budget "experiment" is a failure, explanations should be sought so that the failure may be prevented in the future. Behavioral considerations represent one potential explanation which merits analysis. This might take place at individual, small-group, organizational, and even at societal levels. At the individual level, motivational explanations could be explored using either process or content types of theories. Expectancies and Maslovian hierarchies may also be relevant. At the small-group level, budget failure might be explained by leadership style or interaction patterns. At the organizational level, questions about position, role, and role conflict might be raised. All of these constitute a missing dimension in our understanding of the budget process.

Green responded by defending his pessimism. While he agreed that the issues raised were important ones, he saw no evidence to suggest that behavioral research in the 1970s will be any more successful in solving these issues than it was in the 1960s. Green's point was reinforced by another person who believed that little of substance or operational benefit has come from our inventory of behavioral research. If this disappointing result is to change in the future, some new approach or insight must appear.

The session concluded with a consensus that behavioral issues are important ones in accounting. However, if progress in this area is to be made, it must be made by accountants trained in the behavioral sciences, but working with behavioral scientists. The assumption is that behavioral scientists are not themselves motivated to explore accounting issues and that accountants do not have sufficient expertise to undertake such studies independently.

HISTORICAL PERSPECTIVE ON BEHAVIORAL ACCOUNTING RESEARCH

Robert H. Ashton
Professor of Accounting
New York University

The relationship between accounting and decision making dominates contemporary accounting research. This relationship takes many forms. Accountants supply information to decision makers within organizations for use in operating, financing, and performance-evaluation decisions. They supply information to external parties for use in investment portfolio, credit granting and other types of decisions. Accountants themselves make decisions about which information to produce and supply via their choices among alternative information systems. Independent auditors make a broad range of judgments and decisions when performing an audit and reporting its results.

A substantial amount of research on judgment and decision making in accounting contexts has been conducted. The most extensive and important part of this work is known as human information processing research. The goals of this research involve understanding, evaluating, and improving decision making as it relates to accounting.

Human information processing research in accounting is introduced in this chapter by providing some historical perspective on the broader area of behavioral accounting research. The emergence of behavioral accounting research, the predominance of studies relating to decision making and budgeting/control systems, and two significant problems of "early" behavioral accounting research are considered. Then, two important paradigms of human information processing research, which overcome these two problems to a great extent, are briefly described. Finally, the scope and organization of this book are explained.

1.1 HISTORICAL PERSPECTIVE

Knowing the history of a discipline can be very useful in terms of understanding and interpreting the current status of that discipline. One problem in attempting to communicate history is that the account is influenced by the particular viewpoint adopted by the reporter. Another problem is that historical reports tend to make the events and trends of the past appear more orderly and purposeful than was actually the case when those events and trends unfolded. Subject to these problems, however, historical information can be instructive. Therefore, this section offers a brief historical perspective on the subject matter of this book.

1.1.1 Behavioral Accounting Research

Human information processing research in accounting is a subset of behavioral accounting research. While the origins of behavioral accounting research can be traced at least to the early 1950s, few empirical or experimental studies appeared before the middle 1960s. Two monographs on budgeting and management control systems, both written by nonaccountants, were published in the 1950s [Argyris, 1952; Simon, Guetzkow, Kozmetsky, and Tyndall, 1954]. Within a few years, these works were considered major contributions to the "human side" of accounting, although some dissenters to this view existed (see, e.g., Anthony's [1960] critique of Argyris' work).

Carl Devine is recognized as the first accounting researcher to emphasize behavioral aspects of accounting. In one of his published papers, Devine [1960] introduced his concern for behavioral issues in this way (p. 394):

> Let us now turn to that part of accounting which is related directly to the psychological reactions of those who consume accounting output or are caught in its threads of control. On balance it seems fair to conclude that accountants seem to have waded through their relationships to the intricate psychological network of human activity with a heavy-handed crudity that is beyond belief. Some degree of crudity may be excused in a new discipline, but failure to recognize that much of what passes as accounting theory is hopelessly entwined with unsupported behavior assumptions is unforgiveable.

Devine mentioned several behavioral issues that typically were ignored by accountants, as well as some research methods that might be useful for investigating behavioral aspects of accounting. In addition, Devine's concern for behavioral issues is evident throughout many of his privately-distributed essays. For example, in "Some Behavioral Aspects of Accounting" [1962], he recognized some potential implications for accounting of the work of the psychologist Egon Brunswik. At that time, Brunswik's work was just beginning to be appreciated in psychology, and several years later it would serve as a paradigm for human information processing research in accounting.

The popularity of behavioral accounting research increased from the middle 1960s to the early 1970s, and the area seemed to include a potpourri of research topics. The two major topics were the impact of budgets and management control systems on the attitudes and performance of individuals who were subject to their control, and the impact of accounting information on the decision-making behavior of internal and external users. Two other topics that often were considered part of behavioral accounting were human resource accounting and social responsibility accounting. Some of the research in these two areas concerned the impact of human resource or social responsibility information on decision making, and might be considered a subset of the decision-making studies mentioned above. Still other topics that were considered by some to constitute behavioral accounting research were sociological and socio-psychological aspects of working in public accounting firms, turnover in public accounting firms, personality characteristics of accountants and users of accounting information, and almost any accounting-related issue for which individuals' attitudes or opinions were sought.

During the late 1960s and early 1970s, some accounting researchers wanted to "provide direction" and "establish boundaries" for behavioral accounting research. This desire is typified by a 1970 article by Hofstedt and Kinard, who advocated "an overall strategy for approaching future research and a means whereby topics and methods may be selected . . . ." (p. 39). While some observers found this to be a "galling" suggestion [Green, 1973, p. 103], it was not without some supporters because of the proliferation of research topics and methods that were considered part of behavioral accounting research. A related impetus for providing direction for behavioral accounting research was the "real world" orientation of such research. Many observers wanted to see this orientation strengthened further by increasing the external validity of behavioral accounting studies. They were especially concerned that behavioral accounting research have practical implications, and the way to insure this was thought to be to emphasize "realistic" research issues and situations. This emphasis was accompanied by a disdain for laboratory experiments and for using student subjects as decision makers.

An integral part of the concern for establishing boundaries was the effort to define behavioral accounting research. The AAA Committee on Behavioral Science Content of the Accounting Curriculum [1971] approached this task by first attempting to define behavioral science. The Committee argued that research had to satisfy two criteria to be part of behavioral science: "First, it must ultimately deal with human behavior . . . . Second, the research must be accomplished in a 'scientific manner' " (p. 248). The importance of *science* in behavioral science was elaborated by the Committee (p. 248):

> The differences between the deliberate research activities of the behavioral scientist and the casual observations and conclusions of the sophisticated layman are mainly matters of procedure or method. They have to do with how clearly and precisely a person formulates his concepts, how carefully and systematically he makes and records observations, and how rigorously he reasons from data to conclusions.
>
> The objective of behavioral science is to understand, explain and predict human behavior; that is, to establish generalizations about human behavior that are supported by empirical evidence collected in an impersonal way by procedures that are completely open to review and replication and capable of verification by other interested scholars.

Hofstedt and Kinard [1970] approached the definition issue more directly. They defined behavioral accounting research as " . . . the study of the behavior of accountants or the behavior of nonaccountants as they are influenced by accounting functions and reports" (p. 43). According to this definition, behavioral accounting research encompassed three areas — the behavior of accountants, the influence of the accounting function on behavior, and the influence of accounting information on those receiving that information. While Hofstedt and Kinard discussed all three areas, most of their attention was devoted to the third.

In contrast to Hofstedt and Kinard and the 1971 Committee, later writers contended that trying to define behavioral accounting research was not likely to be productive. For example, Bruns [1973, p. 124] maintained that "the question of how broadly behavioral accounting should be defined will have to be solved on an ad hoc basis by each researcher." Similarly, the AAA Committee on the Relationship of Behavioral Science to Accounting [1974, p. 127] argued that "it seems improper to worry very much about the 'correct' boundaries; they will evolve and be refined without help from writers of editorials or committee reports."

The extent to which editorials influenced behavioral accounting research is difficult to determine. However, the discipline did begin to assume certain characteristics. Hofstedt's 1975 survey found that the great majority of behavioral accounting studies that appeared in three "academic" journals over the period 1964 to 1975 was devoted to two areas: decision making and budgeting/control systems. More than half the 90 articles he identified concerned the impact of accounting information on decision making. Hofstedt's "crude definition" (p. 28) of behavioral accounting research excluded "nominally behavioral topics which bear only a tenuous link with a more fundamental social science — e.g., human resource accounting and social cost accounting; and . . . behavioral studies of accountants *qua* accountants — e.g., studies of the causes of turnover in CPA firms." It also excluded attitude and opinion surveys. The predominance in the literature of studies concerning the use of accounting information in decision making continued throughout the 1970s.

While research activity in behavioral accounting increased substantially during the time period covered by Hofstedt's survey, several observers began to voice reservations about this type of research. Two related problems became apparent. One was what the 1974 Committee called the quality control problem: " . . . as behavioral accounting has evolved, anything behavioral has been considered 'good.' Empirical behaviorism, however theory-free or ill-conceived, has been an almost sure ticket to success in accounting circles" (p. 130). The Committee argued that

> . . . we can no longer justify slipshod work by "relevance" or "applicability to *real* problems." The word slipshod is used advisedly. Our behavioral research is simply not conducted in accordance with the standards required of *applied* behavioral research in other areas. (p. 130)

The quality control problem arose, in part, because of insufficient knowledge of behavioral research methodologies — by those who attempted to do behavioral accounting research and those who evaluated it. The 1971 Committee's emphasis on the *science* in behavioral science had not been heeded by many academic accountants.

Insufficient knowledge of the *content* of behavioral science — in addition to the methodologies — also contributed to the quality control problem. A definitional rule-of-thumb appeared to be: If it's not "quantitative," then it must be "behavioral." While few researchers would have attempted quantitative research in accounting without thorough preparation, lack of preparation was seldom considered an obstacle for doing behavioral research. Knowledge of statistics and experimental design often was mistaken for knowledge of behavioral science. Inadequate preparation in the methodologies and content of behavioral science was detrimental to the development and acceptance of behavioral accounting research.

The other problem that plagued behavioral accounting research during the 1960s and early 1970s was the lack of theoretical frameworks to guide the research efforts. Some have referred to this problem as the lack of formal models. Without some type(s) of theory(ies) or model(s), each behavioral accounting study stood alone. Hypothesis formulation was precarious. It was difficult to anticipate the effects of independent variables or to know which variables to control in a particular study. The results of different studies were difficult to integrate.

Several observers commented on the lack of theoretical frameworks in behavioral accounting research. The 1974 Committee observed that " . . . too much of behavioral accounting research has consisted of hunting and tracking something without knowing what it was . . . [B]ehavioral accounting research has too much empirical data and too few formal models. Adding further empirical data to the existing, unrelated mountain of bits of information will not help progress toward a science of behavioral accounting, and may in fact actually hinder such progress" (p. 135). Hofstedt [1975] was particularly adamant: "[Behavioral accounting research] still suffers from a dearth of experimental controls, lack of replication and, most vital, from a near-complete detachment from any theory which would enable one to generalize beyond the immediate experiment" (p. 40). "[Behavioral accounting research] did not seem to do much to exploit the vast and rich intellectual heritage of the underlying social sciences . . . ." (p. 30).

These criticisms were directed toward the entire area of behavioral accounting research. Other observers offered similar critiques of the subset of studies dealing with the use of accounting information in decision making. The lack of a theory of users' information processing behavior was emphasized by Birnberg [1973]: " . . . we lack at least a tentative theory of how accounting information is processed by users. Such a theory once developed would permit the generation of new studies. These studies could explore the implications of the theory and investigate inconsistencies between the model and isolated studies" (p. 130). Dyckman, Gibbins, and Swieringa [1978] made a similar point in 1975:[1] "First and foremost, some theory, some model of the decision process is needed to support the empirical results found and to suggest reasonable and useful research projects . . . . Whether such a theory is developed from psychology (information-processing models, conflict and dissonance theory, attitude formation and change models) or from economics (information economics, market choice and marginal analysis, capital asset pricing) is not the critical issue. Indeed, separate theories may all prove productive" (p. 89).

Probably the harshest critique of decision-making studies at the individual level was that of Gonedes and Dopuch:

> . . . we would argue that if a researcher has no conceptual framework or perspective (however tentative) bearing on what he is investigating and if he has no ideas (however tentative) on the linkage(s) between his specific project and his ultimate object(s) of analysis, then he ought not to be doing his "research" until those issues have been attacked. Otherwise, he can hardly claim that he is dealing with a simplified model because he has no perspective on what it is that he is simplifying. Indeed, if he is in this position it is not clear that he can even design an experiment [1974b, p. 167].

Writers who wanted more theory in behavioral accounting research seemed to be calling for "middle-range" theories instead of one all-encompassing theory of

---

[1] This paper was widely available in 1975, although a publication lag delayed its publication until 1978.

behavior.[3] In addition, they seemed to recognize that relevant behavioral theories were beginning to emerge. Gonedes and Dopuch referred optimistically to emerging theories of human judgment:

> . . . with specific reference to the lab/field studies, it is important to note that substantial theoretical building blocks can be found in the behavioral literature. This is especially the case in the area of human judgment and human information usage [1974b, pp. 167-68].

1.1.2 Human Information Processing Research

The "substantial theoretical building blocks . . . in the area of human judgment and human information usage" referred to by Gonedes and Dopuch had been discovered by a small number of accounting researchers in the early 1970s. Much of the research in this area had been guided by two paradigms — the lens paradigm and the subjectively expected utility (SEU) paradigm.

Briefly, the lens paradigm emphasizes the construction of linear models as representations of the information-processing activities of decision makers. It further emphasizes the accuracy of intuitive decisions relative to those prescribed by formal models, the extent to which the intuitive decisions of expert decision makers agree, and several means of improving both accuracy and agreement. The SEU paradigm, like the lens paradigm, also entails decision modeling and it, too, emphasizes the relationship between intuitive decisions and those prescribed by formal models. In addition, the SEU paradigm explicitly focuses on the assessment, revision, and use of probabilities in decision making.

The lens and SEU approaches to the study of human information processing may be considered paradigms in the sense that they " . . . define the legitimate problems and methods of a research field . . . , [have] attract[ed] an enduring group of adherents away from competing modes of scientific activity [and are]

[3] For elaboration on middle-range theories, see Merton [1967] in sociology, Weick [1974] in organization theory, and Becker [1969] and Caplan [1972] in accounting

sufficiently open-ended to leave all sorts of problems for the redefined group of practitioners to resolve" [Kuhn, 1962, p. 10]. If, like Reynolds [1971, Chapter 2], one makes distinctions among Kuhn paradigms, paradigms, and paradigm variations, then the lens and SEU approaches would likely occupy one of the latter two categories. According to Reynolds, Kuhn paradigms entail radically new conceptualizations, or "world views," of phenomena associated with the paradigm, as well as dramatic new research methodologies or strategies; paradigms represent definite shifts in orientation, but less than "scientific revolutions"; paradigm variations involve refinements of details or variations in emphasis within a Kuhn paradigm or paradigm. Reynolds maintains that most theories or orientations in the social sciences can be considered paradigms, and he offers utility theory and information-processing models of cognition as examples. Another view would hold that these two examples (and, similarly, the lens and SEU approaches) are variations on a single paradigm.

Relying on well-developed paradigms for conceptual and methodological guidance offers substantial advantages for behavioral decision making research in accounting. The two major problems of earlier behavioral accounting research — the lack of theoretical frameworks and inadequate quality control — have been alleviated to a significant extent, in the area of human information processing research, by the introduction of the lens and SEU paradigms. In addition, two important corollaries to the introduction of these paradigms are (1) a retreat from the overriding devotion to external validity and an increased emphasis on the internal validity of behavioral decision making research in accounting,[4] and (2) a recognition that some form of training in the methodologies and content of behavioral science is essential for high-quality behavioral decision making research in accounting.

---

[4] Campbell and Stanley [1963] provide an excellent discussion of internal and external validity.

References for

"Historical Perspective on Behavioral Accounting Research"

Anthony, R. N., "Distinguishing Good From Not-So-Good Accounting Research," Proceedings of the 22nd Annual Institute on Accounting (Ohio State University, 1960), pp. 65-75.

Argyris, C., The Impact of Budgets on People (Controllership Foundation, 1952).

Becker, S., "The Behavior of 'Behavioral' Accountants," in R. R. Sterling and W. F. Bentz, eds., Accounting in Perspective: Contributions to Accounting Thought by Other Disciplines (South-Western, 1971), pp. 69-78.

Birnberg, J. G., "Comments on a Paper by David Green," in N. Dopuch and L. Revsine, eds., Accounting Research 1960-70: A Critical Evaluation (University of Illinois, 1973), pp. 126-32.

Bruns, W. J., "Comments on a Paper by David Green," in N. Dopuch and L. Revsine, eds., Accounting Research 1960-1970: A Critical Evaluation (University of Illinois, 1973), pp. 116-25.

Campbell, D. T. and J. C. Stanley, Experimental and Quasi-Experimental Designs for Research (Rand-McNally, 1963).

Caplan, E. H., "Accounting Research as an Information Source for Theory Construction," Supplement to The Accounting Review (1972), pp. 437-44.

Committee on Behavioral Science Content of The Accounting Curriculum, "Report of the Committee on Behavioral Science Content of the Accounting Curriculum," Supplement to The Accounting Review (1971), pp. 247-85.

Committee on the Relationship of Behavioral Science and Accounting, "Report of the Committee on the Relationship of Behavioral Science and Accounting," Supplement to The Accounting Review (1974), pp. 127-39.

Devine, C. T., "Research Methodology and Accounting Theory Formation," The Accounting Review (July 1960), pp. 387-99.

Devine, C. T., "Some Behavioral Aspects of Accounting," Essays in Accounting Theory, Vol. 1 (1962), pp. 70-85.

Dyckman, T. R., M. Gibbins and R. J. Swieringa, "Experimental and Survey Research in Financial Accounting: A Review and Evaluation," in A. R. Abdel-khalik and T. F. Keller, eds., The Impact of Accounting Research on Practice and Disclosure (Duke University, 1978), pp. 48-105.

Gonedes, N. J. and N. Dopuch, "A Reply," Studies on Financial Accounting Objectives, Supplement to Journal of Accounting Research (1974), pp. 158-69. (b)

Green, D. O., "Behavioral Science and Accounting Research," in N. Dopuch and L. Revsine, eds., Accounting Research 1960-1970: A Critical Evaluation (University of Illinois, 1973), pp. 93-104.

Hofstedt, T. R., "A State-of-the-Art Analysis of Behavioral Accounting Research," Journal of Contemporary Business (Autumn 1975), pp. 27-49.

Hofstedt, T. R. And J. C. Kinard, "A Strategy for Behavioral Accounting Research," The Accounting Review (January 1970), pp. 38-54.

Kuhn, T. S., The Structure of Scientific Revolutions (University of Chicago, 1962).

Merton, R. K., "On Sociological Theories of the Middle Range," in R. K. Merton, ed., On Theoretical Sociology (Free Press, 1967), pp. 39-72.

Reynolds, P. D., A Primer in Theory Construction (Bobbs-Merril, 1971).

Simon, H. A., H. Guetzkow, G. Kozmetsky and G. Tyndall, Centralization vs. Decentralization in Organizing the Controller's Department (Controllership Foundation, 1954).

Weick, K. E., "Middle Range Theories of Social Systems," Behavioral Science (November 1974), pp. 357-67.